HOPE FOR HAITI

HOPE FOR HAITI

by
Eleanor Workman

with
JoAnne Cramberg

Tulsa, Oklahoma

Unless otherwise indicated, all Scripture quotations are taken from *The King James Version* of the Bible.

All Scripture quotations marked NIV are taken from *The Holy Bible: New International Version*. Copyright © 1973, 1978, 1984 by The International Bible Society. Used by permission of Zondervan Bible Publishers.

All Scripture quotations marked NKJV are taken from *The New King James Version* of the Bible. Copyright © 1979, 1980, 1982, Thomas Nelson, Inc., Publishers.

The names of some persons mentioned have been changed to protect their privacy.

Hope for Haiti
ISBN 1-892728-05-2

P. O. Box 634545
Margate, Florida 33063-4545

Published by
PHOS PUBLISHING, INC.
P. O. Box 690447
Tulsa, Oklahoma 74169-0447

Printed in the United States of America.

Contents

Contents

Acknowledgements

To properly acknowledge all the individuals who have helped the ministry of Christian Haitian Outreach would be impossible for me. I wish I could do that, but it would require listing literally hundreds of names. Over these many years God has provided countless friends, co-workers and pastors to help me, and I thank them from the bottom of my heart for all they have done. Without their help CHO could never have become what it is today.

The most important person I wish to acknowledge is Jesus. He is the One Who saved me, delivered me from despair, and gave me the opportunity to share His love with the people of Haiti. All that we do in this ministry is done as unto Him, for He has told us, "Whatever you did for one of the least of these brothers of mine, you did for me" (Matthew 25:40 NIV).

May all of us remain faithful until He calls us home and we hear Him say, "Well done, thou good and faithful servant" (Matthew 25:21).

Eleanor Workman

HOPE FOR HAITI

Foreword by Ruthanne Garlock

On that steamy July 10, 1919 in Montclair, New Jersey, when Eleanor was born, no one could have dreamed that the Tuells' fourth child would one day become a missionary, and eventually be known as "Mom" to hundreds of Haitian children. Nor that God would use her to inspire many hundreds more to "be His hand extended" by helping in all kinds of ways to minister to these needy ones.

Back in the early 1980's my husband John came home one day with an enthusiastic report about the visiting missionary who'd spoken to students in his missions class that morning at Christ For The Nations Institute, where he was an instructor. Eleanor Workman had inspired and challenged the students with her account of becoming a full-time missionary at age fifty-two — overcoming enormous obstacles to establish a school and an orphanage for the poor and abandoned children of Haiti.

When we invited her to our home for dinner the next evening she shared more stories of how she founded Christian Haitian Outreach. I was struck by her deep love for the Lord, her strong faith in God to do the impossible, and her singleness of purpose to help the Haitian people — especially the babies and children. Since our "divine appointment" that day I've counted her as one of my dearest friends.

Soon my husband and I made our first trip to Haiti to participate in the annual July Convention hosted by Christian Haitian Outreach. John taught workshops for the dozens of pastors attending the event while I became better acquainted with Eleanor and the daily routines at the orphanage. Amazed at how this woman was able to do so much with so few resources, I went home determined to get other people involved in the ministry of CHO. Over the next few years I organized missions trips for three different work teams to go to Haiti. My own mom went on one of those trips, and my mother-in-law — who was eighty-four at the time — went on another. Both of them loved the experience.

Many wonderful CHO experiences stand out in my memory, such as:

— introducing her to pastor friends who now love and support the ministry...

— going with Eleanor and her workers to bury little Verdy in the local cemetery...

— bringing one of her babies to the U.S. to receive medical treatment.

But the highlight of my many adventures with this remarkable woman was in January 1987 when a small group of teachers and medical volunteers accompanied me to Haiti. We concluded the week there by going on an outreach trip to the mountains. Following is a portion of the report of that trip, written just after we returned:

> At 5:00 on a Saturday morning the bus left the compound loaded with supplies and workers (some American and some Haitian). After a grueling five-hour journey we arrived at the

mountain community called Bainet, and set up a makeshift clinic on the front porch of the house of a CHO worker who lived in this region. We could see no other houses and no people — only tropical wilderness. But when one of the Haitian workers blew a conch shell to summon the people, scores of them suddenly appeared and crowded around the porch to receive medical help.

Working nonstop for the next several hours, we ministered to their needs as best we could with one doctor, two nurses and several helpers to dispense medications, pass out Creole New Testaments, and witness to the people one-to-one. Many coming through the clinic had told us, "I want to be free from fear." Finally one of the witnessing workers came to the medical team and said, "We've got to have some help — there are just too many people out there wanting to get saved!"

Since we were running out of daylight and medicine anyway, we closed down the clinic and asked Eleanor to come share a gospel message with the whole crowd. No one had gone home, and at least three hundred people were now crowded into the yard in front of the house. They'd never seen such an event in their community, so no one wanted to leave.

With an interpreter by her side, Eleanor used the porch for a pulpit. Her voice rang out over the mountainside as the Holy Spirit anointed her to proclaim the Good News — the timeless message that Jesus is the only antidote for fear. Here in this voodoo stronghold, we team members could literally feel the power of the Holy Spirit moving upon that crowd as we prayed and Eleanor preached. At the close of the message at least one hundred of them raised their hands and prayed to receive Christ into their hearts.

After our host served a Haitian meal of wild turkey, rice, and fried plantain, we hurried to load up and begin our return trip before dark. But while carrying supplies back down the mountain to the bus, we met more people just arriving. We offered them all that we had left — a small quantity of vitamins and aspirin.

"We appreciate the medicine," they said to Eleanor, "but someone told us they heard about Jesus up here, and that's why we came. Would you tell us how we can find Jesus?" Eleanor gave them a shortened version of her earlier message, and soon was praying with the group. We rejoiced that several more Haitians were born into the Kingdom before our bus finally pulled away to begin the long ride back to the CHO compound. And we all came home hopelessly "hooked" on missions.

Literally hundreds of CHO friends have gone to Haiti to help with the work over these years. Their trips surely have made a great impact upon each one of them, just as my first trip, and especially that 1987 trip, influenced me so deeply. Various friends who accompanied me on such trips have told me years later that meeting

Eleanor Workman and having their own personal Haiti experience had forever changed them.

As all who know her will affirm, music has been a big part of Eleanor's ministry from her earliest years. No doubt the song which best epitomizes her life is "Let Me Touch Him," and hearing her sing it with her rich contralto voice always moves me to tears. These words of "her song" have touched the hearts of thousands of people in missions conferences, church meetings, Bible studies, and gatherings at the CHO compound in Haiti:

Let Me Touch Him

Let me touch Him, let me touch Jesus.
Let me touch Him as He passes by.
Then when I shall reach out to touch others,
They shall know Him, they shall live, and not die.

Oh, to be His hand extended,
Reaching out to the oppressed!
Let me touch Him; let me touch Jesus,
So that others may know and be blessed.

I was straying so far from Jesus;
I was lonely, had no peace within.
Then the hand of my Saviour touched me.
Now I'm reaching to others in sin.

Oh, to be His hand extended,
Reaching out to the oppressed!
Let me touch Him; let me touch Jesus,
So that others may know and be blessed.

— Vep Ellis*

Introduction

Haiti: a land filled with the darkness of witchcraft, a beautiful island discovered by Christopher Columbus in December of 1492. Indians lived there at the time, but most died off from disease or were killed by invading armies. Haiti and the Dominican Republic, which share the same island, were once owned by the Spanish.

In 1697 the western third of the island was ceded to France by Spain and during the 18th century the population grew rapidly. At one time the island became the most prosperous New World colony, exporting sugar, coffee, cocoa, indigo and cotton. It was also a great slave trading post. As the slave population quickly increased, it soon outnumbered white settlers.

Wars and revolutions became commonplace. In 1804 the Haitians gained their freedom from the French. Ninety percent of the population now consisted of Africans, and blacks began to rule their new possession.

From those early days of freedom until today, Haiti's culture remains almost unchanged. Newspapers from years ago report the same hopes and dreams for a tiny nation as do the reports today. U.S. military intervention has somewhat changed the face of this country, because they have made some inroads with building hospitals, schools and good roads in some areas. Today Haiti's small land mass — about the size of the state of

Maryland — holds over seven million people.

In 1994 Haiti's first democratically elected president was reinstated to office after three years in exile. At this writing a newly-elected president has taken office.

But no political system has been able to produce economic miracles and end the abject misery in this country. Some U.S. State Department workers have privately reported the HIV rate to be over 80 percent. Half of the children die before they reach the age of five from starvation, malnutrition, or exposure to disease and inclemete weather. They sleep on the ground, under trees, or wherever they can. Many children are forced to beg and most of them work for their food. They must carry water on their heads at four and five years old; they baby-sit, run errands, and clean houses. They have no childhood.

Three out of four Haitians are illiterate. More than half of the workforce is unemployed or at best works only a few days each month.

Voodoo worship is pervasive in Haiti's culture. One leader proclaimed, "Voodoo is the soil of the nation." But the soil has been good only for burying the dead in this country, declared by some to be the most religious in the Western Hemisphere. But it is also the poorest nation in the Western Hemisphere.

Defying death and devil worship for the past twenty-five years, a petite powerhouse — Eleanor "Mom" Workman — has been about the Father's business in Haiti. She has rescued hundreds of children from garbage heaps and street corners — feeding, healing, restoring innocent victims and teaching the gospel of

Christ to tiny, brilliant minds caught in the crossfire of satanic influence in a nation suffering the consequences of sin.

The story is too great to be told in one small volume. However, within these pages I will introduce you to Eleanor, this 5-foot stick of dynamite, who is blowing holes in the enemy's stronghold — preserving and raising up righteous seed to carry the message of the Savior into the next generation. While in her mid-fifties she took on the greatest challenge of her life, sold everything and under God's direction, moved to Haiti to rescue the perishing.

You will also meet some of the children. Exceptional and miraculous stories of lives rescued from death, now bringing life and joy into the hearts and homes of others.

Her story will amaze you, encourage you and move you to tears. Prepare to fall in love with this woman of faith and prayer. You will be challenged to know thy God, be strong, and do great exploits (Daniel 11:32).

JoAnne Cramberg

1
Humble Entrance — Holy Closure

When he brings out his own sheep, he goes before them; and the sheep follow him, for they know his voice.

John 10:4 NKJV

My early childhood memories while growing up in a small town in New Jersey are of longing to feel secure and loved by my parents — especially by my father. But because he was an alcoholic who seldom fulfilled his paternal responsibility, life was difficult for all of us — my mother, my four sisters and me, and my only brother. From the time I was little, my heart was full of hatred toward this negligent father.

Determined to hold the family together, Mom kept us in church. She told my sisters and me that because God had blessed us with the ability to sing we must use our gifts for Him, even though there was no money for music lessons. So from the time I was young we sang together in church.

We were raised with "the Bible and the belt," as Mom always carried her strap to church with her just in case. Either the fear of God or the fear of the strap kept me in check until I surrendered my life to the Lord at the age of fifteen. The proof of my salvation came when I realized I now loved the father I had so bitterly resented.

Over the years I found comfort in singing and serving in the church — in fact, it seemed my whole life revolved around the church. In the early days I traveled and sang with evangelistic teams, and later formed and directed award-winning choirs. I loved to see people coming to the Lord and being blessed through gospel music. Yet very often, I was distressed by what had seemed to be a double standard in the church from the time I was a young girl: women were expected to submit without question to the will of the church leaders.

Some of these men had impure, self-seeking motives, and their position of power allowed them to take advantage of those under their authority. Though they were supposed to be answerable to church officials over them, I learned through my own bitter experience that appeals to those men in office usually fell on deaf ears. Many of us in the church suffered abuses too painful to mention because of this double standard. Since my mother lived by the doctrine that we were to "touch not God's anointed," she wouldn't allow me or my sisters to talk about the mistreatment we experienced under this system.

But in spite of chafing under this code of silence, I continued serving in the church, and at age twenty-seven married a man in the congregation — not because I loved him, but because he and the church leaders felt this was God's will. A few months later my husband left his secular job and both of us worked and traveled for a while with an evangelistic team; he was a driver and we sang together. Eventually we settled in the Los

Angeles area. He got a job as a truck driver, and both of us became involved in the music ministry of a large church there.

My husband lived like a man with two faces. Church leaders admired him for his winning personality and exceptional singing ability, regarding him as a talented, godly man. This "public face" as a singer and worker in the church was quite convincing. But from early on in the marriage I knew he was unfaithful, and at home he showed no respect toward me at all. He began drinking heavily, gradually became physically abusive, and frequently ran with other women while on the road with his truck. If I tried to confront him about these things, he would slap me or throw me down on the floor — he even threatened to kill me if I dared to talk to anyone. More than once I had to go conduct choir rehearsal at the church with a split lip or a black eye.

I felt I had no one to turn to since people in the church respected him as a godly man. And my earlier experience of trying to appeal to church authorities about abuses I had suffered — only to be ignored — kept me from doing that again. Of course I knew that not all leaders were corrupt, as I had worked with some true men of God. I finally realized my only recourse was to cry out to God for comfort, strength and deliverance from what seemed to me to be an impossible situation.

It would have been easy for me to slip into the pitfall of self-pity and self-righteousness. But as I learned the value of fasting, God sustained me through days and nights of seeking Him. Though at one time I had held seven positions in the church, I realized that simply being in church — even if you are talented and have a respected title — doesn't save you. Often when you are in the work of the Lord it is quite easy to begin to major in the minor and minor in the major. It doesn't take an anointing to work in the church, but it does take the anointing of the Holy Spirit to truly serve God. How grateful I am that God is very patient with us — He will meet us where we are, then lead us on. He had already begun to speak to my heart about missions, but at that time I could not have imagined what He had in store for me.

Finally my husband left to take a job with a former employer back east, and I never saw him again. At no time did he offer me a penny of support, nor did I seek to obtain a divorce — I simply accepted his leaving as God's intervention and answer to my prayers. (More than twenty-six years later I learned from a member of his family that he had passed away.) I had every assurance that my Heavenly Father would never leave me nor forsake me.

When I was able to obtain a license for taking care of children, I felt this was God's provision to help me keep my home after I was left alone. I purchased beds and cribs and transformed my house into a wonderful day care facility. It seemed I'd been born with a skill for caring for children. I fed them the right things and their health improved. All the children in my place were happy and healthy, and the mothers were thrilled with the care I was providing for their kids.

Although the business was thriving, that still, small voice kept speaking to me about the mission field. I reminded God that by caring for the children I actually was working on a mission field. But the financial burden of the house still was heavy, and it seemed a nagging reminder to me that something just wasn't right. During a difficult financial crisis I began to seek God more diligently than ever before. A twenty-one-day fast birthed in me a quietness and a greater faith-filled confidence in the Lord. Later, I went on an even longer fast to ask for God's direction for my life.

Then one morning while I was busy with menial chores the Lord clearly spoke to my heart: "Sell the house." Through the fasts I had come to know the voice of the Lord as never before, and I knew this was His voice. But His words were a great shock to me, and I just couldn't accept the idea.

"No way, Lord," I instinctively replied. "I need my house. I like it and I want to keep it. Besides, everyone needs a house, and now with my business I can manage it financially."

But every time I began to pray I would hear God saying, "Sell the house." At last I realized He wanted me to trust Him completely for my future, instead of trusting in the security of owning my house. Reluctantly, I agreed to sell if that was what He wanted. But I decided to put out a fleece, thinking I could stump God with a tough one.

"Okay, I will let the realtor know my house is for sale," I told the Lord. "But I will not let him put up a sign, and only one person may look at it. If that one person who looks at my house doesn't buy it, then I don't believe the voice is from You. I will know the devil is trying to cause me to give up my home."

Sure enough, only one person came to look at the house. It was just right for her needs, and her furniture would fit perfectly. She fell in love with the place and bought it, and lived there until her death a few years ago.

After the house sold I shut down the child care business, packed two suitcases to carry with me, and sold or stored all my other belongings. I thought I had made the supreme sacrifice, but God hadn't finished yet. I began receiving invitations to sing for regional meetings of the Full Gospel Business Men's Fellowship, and for Kathryn Kuhlman Crusades. I would drive to and from the nearby meetings in the Los Angeles area in my immaculate, fully-paid-for Cadillac.

Since I wanted to look good for all the public appearances, I went to a place in Hollywood that could individually style an elegant wig for me and make me look like a movie star. I could leave their place looking like I'd just stepped off the cover of a magazine. Although it cost a pricey $300, I thought it was worth it as I sat behind the wheel of my big shiny Coupe de Ville, admiring my appearance in the visor mirror.

One day after leaving the beauty parlor all fixed up for a concert appearance, I was zooming along Harbor Boulevard. Right there in the middle of traffic, the Spirit of God suddenly spoke to my heart. This time His words were even more shocking than when He had told me to sell the house.

"Sell the car," the Lord said.

"No, Lord! I can't do that," I immediately replied. I went on to remind Him, in case He had missed the news, "It is dangerous to ride public buses and trains, and most of my work is at night. I just have to have my car."

God didn't argue. That is not His style. He just

continued to speak, and I continually heard Him saying, "Sell the car." Finally, when I mentioned to friends that my car was for sale, it sold immediately. Everyone knew what great shape the car was in, and they had no problem with my asking price. My last prized possession was now gone.

With the money from the sale of the car still in my handbag, I flew to Phoenix, Arizona, to sing for a Full Gospel Business Men's meeting. As I checked into my room, unpacked and prepared for the meeting, I was overcome with the joy of the Lord. I felt I had given up all my possessions and given my whole life to Jesus. I began to praise God for His faithfulness to me through all the pain and trials, and thank Him that though the enemy had meant those things for evil, He had turned it into good. The surrender was sweet. I was now ready to listen to His voice for direction in my call, and let Him have His way with my life.

2
Ordered Steps

> **Your ears shall hear a word behind you, saying, "This is the way, walk in it," whenever you turn to the right hand or whenever you turn to the left.**
>
> **Isaiah 30:21 NKJV**

After having given up almost all my worldly possessions except my clothing I was completely dependent upon God and learning to walk by faith like never before. Now instead of being wrapped up in my own problems, I was concerned for the lost and needy on the mission field, as well as for those all around me who didn't know the Lord.

A friend had provided a room for me in Los Angeles, not far from the Watts area where dreadful racial riots erupted in the mid-1960's. My heart was heavy as I watched teenagers smashing windows and looting goods from the very stores whose owners had extended credit to their mothers so they could put food on the table. I went into that area and began talking to these young people — telling them about Jesus, and that He could make a difference in their lives.

I did things to show I really cared about them — like buying tickets and taking them to see an ice skating performance, a pleasure they never could have afforded on their own. Although friends warned me about how dangerous this was, I found that I was able to communicate with these youngsters and show them that hatred and rioting only made matters worse. They respected me and listened to me. Some of them made genuine commitments to accept Jesus into their hearts.

About this time I had an opportunity to move to Denver with a friend. She was buying a house there in order to be closer to her sister, and she wanted me to share the place with her and look after it when she had to travel. Someone who knew of the work I had done with young people following the Watts riots recommended me for a position the federal government had just created.

It was a new education policy they were implementing to work with minority students who had either dropped out or flunked out of college, or who were struggling to stay in. Those who committed to working hard and cooperating with the program could receive federal grants to finish their undergraduate work, and to go on and study for the professions such as law or medicine. I got the job as a "watchdog" to counsel and encourage the young people in their studies, and to make sure the government funds were used for the intended purpose. Though some of the students didn't appreciate my diligence to see that they didn't abuse the system, the head of the department was pleased with my work.

While in Denver I got acquainted with missionaries working in Haiti and began raising money to help with their work. I was leading a home Bible study Saturdays and prayer meetings during the week, and we grew from two people to about sixty people in eighteen months. These friends began giving money and goods for Haiti. In order to solicit and dispense these funds properly, two local pastors helped me to establish Christian Haitian Outreach. That was the small beginning of our missions organization, known as CHO, but God has blessed it beyond anything I could have envisioned at the time of its inception.

When I made my first trip to Haiti I saw the tremendous need firsthand — heartbreaking needs that almost overwhelmed me. Any lack I thought I had faded to insignificance by comparison. It made me want to give my whole life to sharing the gospel with these people.

I became especially concerned about children in the poorest areas who were unable to attend school because their parents had no jobs. Education is not mandatory in Haiti, and enrolling in a public school requires paying fees and buying school uniforms. Thus the cost of sending their children to school is out of reach for parents who struggle just to feed their large families.

On one of my trips to Haiti I found a property for sale in a poor suburb of Port-au-Prince some distance from the area where my missionary friends were working. Many children in this neighborhood, called Mariani, were growing up with no education, no knowledge of Jesus, and no future. Determined to try to help them, I asked the Lord to help me make a difference in their lives.

Back in Denver, I began organizing gospel music concerts to raise funds to buy the property. Many friends participated in the project, and through a series of miracles we raised enough money to buy the land. One of the pastors who had helped me with getting CHO registered as a non-profit organization took the money to Haiti and negotiated the property purchase. Now CHO had a permanent location in Haiti.

At this time I was in the fifth year of my government job which God had provided. My hours of working with college young people could be flexible, so this enabled me to work on fund-raising projects and make occasional trips to Haiti. But it became clear that I now had to step out in blind faith once again, just as I had done when I left Los Angeles. I quit the job, and from that time on began dividing my time between raising funds in the U.S. and overseeing the work in Haiti. The lifelong missionary call on my life now began in earnest.

I continued receiving invitations to sing for meetings and conferences, so I would use these opportunities to raise funds for the work in Haiti. When I was invited to sing in Miami, Florida, I made the trip cross-country by bus, never dreaming that on this trip God was arranging divine appointments for me which would change the direction of my life.

It was February, and Miami was bustling with tourists. With no hotel reservations and only $20.00 in my purse I was totally unprepared for this adventure.

After standing on the street outside the bus station for a moment to collect my thoughts, I decided a taxi driver might help me find a hotel with a vacancy. A taxi stopped and I promptly got into the backseat. "Where to, lady?" came the question from the front. "Any motel here in the city," I replied. The driver had no clue I had just arrived by bus from Denver and that I knew nothing about Miami.

"Lady, you are in Miami, and this is the peak season. I can't take you to any hotel unless you have reservations." I didn't realize a hotel room at this time of the year required a six-month advance reservation. I began to talk to myself, reminding my spirit to trust in the Lord and He would show me the way.

The driver must have overheard my prayer. He turned, faced me down and inquired, "You have to do what?" I told the driver if he could not find me a hotel then my Lord would. Certain he had picked up a crazy woman, the driver asked me to get out of the cab and wait on the street corner until the Lord Jesus gave me a hotel. "No, this cab is just fine. I like this one," I responded.

"Lady, you will have to tell me where to go." I replied that I was new to the city and did not know where the hotels were located. "Take me to any hotel — My God will provide, " I blurted out. "Aye, aye, aye," he muttered as he pulled down the lever on the meter.

"God will certainly have to give it to you, because I can't, Lady. I don't have time for this." I reminded him I was a paying customer and that I was staying in that backseat. "I've never had a day like this in my life," I remarked to the driver. "God is going to do it for us!"

Waiting in front of a hotel while the driver went in to check, I noticed through the cab window that there were two women standing near the entrance. Both of them were crying. I rolled down the window and asked the ladies, "Can I help you, are you feeling ill?" They said they were fine except for exhaustion and desperation. They had searched all day for a hotel. They quickly explained they were from Jamaica on a buying trip for their business, and greatly in need of a place to stay.

I invited them into the cab since God was certainly going to show me where there was a place to stay. When the driver returned with bad news, I was not daunted. I was confident my mission at that location had been to pick up the two women from Jamaica.

The driver looked at the crazy woman in the backseat of his cab and now there were more. I told him not to pay any attention to them, just continue looking for a hotel. "Lady, I am going to try only one more place. If this one is full I want every one of you out of my cab."

The newcomers in the backseat stared at one another. They were exhausted and now they had gotten themselves into a strange cab, in a strange city, with a strange woman.

As the taxi driver reentered the vehicle, I felt a strong surge of faith. I was charged with a supernatural power. I felt as though I had power over the cab driver. Proverbs 21:1 came to my mind: "The king's heart is in the hand of the Lord, as the rivers of water: he turneth it whithersoever he will. "

I began to have a personal praise and worship service in the back of that cab as I rejoiced over the goodness and greatness of God. The cab driver interrupted my private praise as the taxi pulled to a stop.

"Ladies, this is the last stop," he said firmly. "Please take your bags with you." My spunky reply came back quickly, "This is fine; all you have to do is go check for us and we will be glad to stay here if this is the place." A minute later the driver returned with a big smile on his face. "They have only one room," he reported. I blurted out, "Praise the Lord, He is so faithful."

The cab fare had mounted to almost fifty dollars. The driver generously agreed to drop the price since I had an inside track with the Lord. "I know if I help you it will mean good luck to me," he said, "I could use some good luck." I explained that good luck had nothing to do with the mercies of God. Jesus would bless him just because He loved him.

"Lady, just give me twelve dollars," he said wearily. Finished with my sermon, I turned to the ladies from Jamaica and told them the fare would be four dollars each. The hotel room proved to be nice but a bit small for three women. The cost was twelve dollars per night. The ladies from Jamaica sat on one bed. I knelt by the other.

When I encouraged the women to join with me in thanking God, one woman declared she did not even know how to pray, while the other one lit up a cigarette. What had God gotten me into? Boldly, I asked them to respect my prayers enough not to smoke while I prayed.

"God, I thank You for Your faithfulness to me in this desperate situation," I spoke aloud. "You are a never-failing God. Thank You for these precious friends You have brought into my life. Please save both of my new friends." Then I threw my hands into the air and praised His name.

They showered and went to bed early, exhausted from the day's unwanted tour of Miami. I awoke at 5 a.m. for my usual time of daily devotions and found my roommates missing. Check-out time was 11 a.m. and I had only sixteen dollars left so again I was standing in need of a miracle.

As if the Lord were unaware of my situation, I spelled it out for Him in prayer, giving Him a detailed accounting. When I quieted myself, I began to listen for God's direction in this dilemma. The thought came to me to look in the yellow pages. I turned to the child care section and my eye stopped on the name, "Golatt." Dialing the number provided in the ad, I felt I was doing exactly what God wanted me to do.

A lady answered the phone and I briefly told her my story of being a missionary traveling on faith. I proceeded to give God the glory for all He had done thus far. Then I boldly asked the lady if she would have space for me to stay for awhile. After a brief pause Mrs. Golatt responded, "Yes, yes, I'll come to where you are."

Later, sitting in the woman's car in front of the hotel, I poured out my heart to her. Mrs. Golatt finally sensed my sincerity and drove me across Miami to a lovely small home. On the way, she shared about her day care center and a church that had been started as a result of the child care.

The meeting I was to sing for was the next night, but my new host had a previous engagement. I not only needed transportation, I needed a pianist to accompany me at the meeting. At 5 p.m. Mrs. Golatt's son arrived to pick up his baby. He was an accomplished pianist and agreed to play for me. We made the perfect team as we rehearsed for the next evening's concert.

What God had prearranged came as no surprise to me. The next evening the anointing of the Holy Spirit fell on both of us as we ministered, "All My Life I Give to the Lord."

3

Anointed and Appointed

The Lord is my strength and my shield;
My heart trusted in Him, and I am helped;
Therefore my heart greatly rejoices,
And with my song I will praise Him.
The Lord is their strength,
And He is the saving refuge of His anointed.

Psalm 28:7-8 NKJV

That night in the Miami meeting a missionary family from Tucson, Arizona — whom I had met before — was in the audience. They were on their way to Haiti a few days later, and invited me to join them. I eagerly said, "Yes." Plans were set, but just before we were to leave, they received a telegram from Haiti telling them not to come. A missionary in the area where they were going had been killed for sharing the gospel.

They also had planned a trip to Jamaica, but they cancelled the entire trip because of their grief over the incident in Haiti. I told them that I was willing to go to Jamaica if they would direct me to some contacts in that country, and then I would go on to Haiti by myself.

In the meeting that night I mentioned that I was going to Jamaica. Afterwards a lady approached me and told me she had a friend in Jamaica, and asked me to call on her when I arrived. She told me her friend had a ministry preaching in the Jamaican prisons, so I took her name, address and telephone number.

I purchased a ticket for Jamaica, boarded the plane, and was on my way to a land that I had never seen before. When I saw the lights of that massive island it looked like multicolored jewels glittering in the heat below. After landing and retrieving my baggage, and clearing immigration and customs, I went outside the terminal and sat down on a bench. "What next, God?" I asked. "I don't have anyone to meet me here." Then I remembered the card in my purse with a missionary's name and phone number written on it.

A taxi driver approached me to see if I needed a ride, but I refused. When the time for the airport to close was only fifteen minutes away, I was still considering my dilemma. Finally one of the workers came and asked if he could help me. I showed him the address on the card and asked if he knew where it was, and he replied "Yes."

He and some other men were just getting off work and they offered to give me a ride. After praying silently for a moment I replied, "Yes, I would appreciate it very much if you would take me to this address." I got in the car with these men whom I did not know, headed for an address of a woman I'd never met. By the time we pulled up in front of a gated house it was just past midnight. I gathered my luggage from the car and tried to open the gate, but it was locked.

"No, no you can't do that," said one of the men in the car. "You have to ring for someone to come to the gate so you can be identified." I rang the bell, and finally a woman opened the door of the house and beckoned for me to come into the courtyard. The men were kind enough to carry my luggage to the front door.

I introduced myself as Eleanor Workman, missionary from the United States, and showed her the card that had her friend's name on it. Recognizing the name, she immediately said with a very pleasant voice, "Please come into my home." She offered me something to eat, but I told her I was more tired than hungry. All she had for sleeping was one small cot, but she shared that with me for the night.

The next morning, a Saturday, as I told her how God had called me into missions work, and she shared with me her story of God's calling, we both rejoiced in the goodness of our Lord. She asked me to go with her the next day to minister at the Hilltop Prison, then to an open-air concert in Kingston. I was thrilled to accept.

Sunday morning we drove through the mountains and farmlands to Hilltop Prison and stopped outside the gates of a huge fortress-like complex. But the armed guards immediately opened the gate for us because they recognized the lady known to them as The Chaplain.

When they led us into a very large room that doubled as recreation hall and meeting room, I was surprised to see there were no seats or benches to sit on. Every prisoner had to stand at attention as we walked into the room. There were all ages, from eleven years to seventy years — young boys and older men all in there together. "All these prisoners will be locked up for the rest of their lives," the missionary told me.

My new friend shared a beautiful message on the Sower and the Seed as all the prisoners listened intently. "Up until now we've had no music," she announced. "But today we are privileged to have a missionary from the United States who will sing for us." I stepped forward and gave a brief testimony of God's saving grace in my own life. I sang that morning in the Hilltop Prison with a special anointing from the Holy Spirit — "Throw out the lifeline, Throw out the lifeline, Someone is sinking today...." I sang a few more songs, then the missionary gave an altar call. Several men and boys with tears in their eyes came forward for salvation. I taught the prisoners a song, and when we left that big room they were still singing, "Oh, how I love Jesus."

As we drove out through the gates we could still hear their voices praising God in the only freedom they will ever know — freedom from sin. My life was changed that day when I saw true freedom come to men who would live the rest of their lives behind bars. We drove slowly so we could hear their singing as long as possible. Finally at the bottom of the hill we could no longer hear their voices. But for the rest of the day, I could not get the sound of the prisoners' singing out of my head.

That evening when we arrived at the concert held by a singer from England, the place was packed with people from all over the island. My friend sent a note to him introducing me as a singing missionary from the United States. He acknowledged me and invited me to sing a couple of songs, then he announced that I had an album that could be purchased at the close of the service.

As my friend was taking orders for the albums I noticed a family from India nearby, dressed in traditional East Indian attire. "We would like one of your albums but we don't have any money," the older lady said.

"That's O.K. I'll be glad to give you an album," I told her. I had only been able to sell eight albums, so I decided I may as well give them away. She offered to bring me the money the next day, so I gave her the address of this precious lady who had taken me in. The next evening the Indian lady came to the house and handed me five dollars, but before she left she invited me to stay at their home for awhile, and I accepted. I became close friends with her and her daughters, and one of them ended up accompanying me to Haiti.

A few days later, as Laraine and I left for Haiti early one morning while most of Jamaica was still asleep, my soul was filled with praises for my King.

We arrived in Haiti without incident, and found a place to stay not far from the CHO property — which at the time was just an empty lot covered with weeds and rubbish. I told Laraine I felt the Lord wanted us to start the school right away.

"We can't start a school without a building," she said.

"All we need is children," I answered.

So we set up a temporary school under a tree on one corner of the lot. We invited a few children from families around the property, and the very first day twenty kids from four to thirteen years old came. These were the poorest of the poor — kids who had only rags for clothes, so they could not attend a public school.

With the dirt serving as a "blackboard" and a sharp rock substituting for chalk, the first lesson began — the English alphabet. We couldn't speak Creole, the language of the common people in Haiti, but we managed to communicate, and Laraine quickly began to pick up the language as she worked with the children.

Our first students were so eager to learn, most of them mastered the alphabet within a week. Before long I was able to purchase a blackboard which we leaned against the tree, and we also purchased chalk. Our portable, makeshift school probably would not have impressed the education experts. But I was confident we were obeying God with this very humble beginning that was making a difference in these children's lives.

Every morning we would go purchase food for the students because some of them were so poor they would go days without eating. Some would find scraps of food in the city dump, often with bugs crawling on it, but they would brush off their morsel and keep on eating. When word spread that we were feeding the children, more began coming to our school to get something to eat.

I knew we needed to take steps to fence the property and erect a building, so I left Laraine in Haiti and returned to Denver to meet with some friends and discuss my school in Haiti. More gospel music concerts and missions meetings followed. As soon as we had sufficient funds, we erected a cinder-block wall around the property. Now we could bring the school children into the compound where they would be safe, even though we didn't yet have a building.

Thus began what became a way of life for me — raising funds in the U.S. for the work in Haiti, and overseeing the development of the property as God enabled us to begin building needed facilities.

I was thrilled to get back to Haiti to work with the children in the school — that was where I found my greatest joy. God blessed our efforts every day because we were caring for the poor, and the school grew so fast I didn't have time to cook the food and care for the children. Finally we hired a cook to prepare the meals. Then we discovered that some of the children attending our school were sick. Fever, worms and bloodshot eyes were some of the symptoms of sickness, causing them to be very tired with no desire to learn.

At the beginning, when we had asked those first twenty children "Who is Jesus?" we got many different answers. Some thought He was the Easter bunny, and one thought He was the President of the United States. No one really knew. But we began teaching about Jesus along with the alphabet and math — feeding their spirits, as well as their minds and bodies.

We taught them that Jesus is the Son of God Who loves them, and that He also has power to heal. I told them the same God Who saves is also the God Who heals their bodies. We began laying hands on them and praying for them as the Bible teaches us. Before long some of the children began to show signs of improvement and eventually were made whole by the power of God. As a result they became more alert and eager to learn their lessons and their learning capacity increased. It reminded me of Daniel when he turned down the king's rich food and chose to eat his own simple food, and then proved to be smarter in learning than the ones who ate the king's food.

As more children began attending the school, we needed more food. So we purchased big iron pots and charcoal stoves to produce greater quantities of beans and rice or whatever we could find.

I continued to go in and out of Haiti, raising funds. At the same time, my friend who had bought the house in Denver was becoming more and more involved with ministry in Haiti. Eventually she sold the Denver property and bought a small home in Margate, Florida, not far from Miami. She allowed me to use the place to establish a headquarters office for CHO to keep in contact with supporters who had promised to help us in Haiti. This became my home while in the U.S., and also allowed us to receive visitors going to and coming from Haiti, as the place is about an hour's drive from the Miami airport.

God provided workers to help me take care of the office work in Margate, as I was on the road almost continually. With all the travel I rarely stayed in a motel. When I considered the cost of a motel room, and realized how much food that could buy for the children in Haiti, I would ask the Lord to provide someone who would open their home to me. God never failed me, and by staying in people's homes I made many new friends who were willing to help with the work. Every place where I stayed the people treated me royally, feeding me and giving me a place to sleep. When I awoke early in the morning I would receive a good breakfast and a prayer, then take off to the next appointment.

My adventure in faith was becoming more challenging day by day, but God continually proved His faithfulness to me. Every problem I had to face and trust Him to solve for me became the training ground for what lay yet ahead.

4
Abandoned Babies

When my father and my mother forsake me,
Then the Lord will take care of me.

Psalm 27: 10 NKJV

Providing schooling for Haitian children whose families couldn't afford to send them to government schools was part of God's plan for CHO. But I knew there was more. I was concerned about the many babies who were abandoned because the mother had no means of caring for the child, or because she had died while giving birth. I contacted Haiti's Social Welfare Department and told them our organization was willing to take in such abandoned children if their office would refer them to us.

Not long after that a doctor friend of ours found an emaciated mother and her twin babies living on a garbage heap. The woman had been evicted from her little hut because she couldn't pay the three-dollars-a-month rent. When the doctor took the six-week-old infants to Social Welfare and told us about the case, I sent a worker to check on the babies and we tried to help the mother. The welfare office released the infants to us, and before she died the mother signed them over to me. But she died knowing Jesus as her Savior, and knowing her babies would be cared for. Those twins actually were the beginning of the CHO orphanage.

News about our orphanage was spreading rapidly. After we'd had the twins for a short time, I received a surprising call one Friday from the Social Welfare office in downtown Port-au-Prince asking me to come in for an appointment. When I went to talk to the workers there, they told me they had fourteen sick, abandoned babies at the hospital, and asked if I would take them. I readily agreed, although for all practical purposes there was no way I could house or care for fourteen sick infants. I rushed home from my meeting and chose six women to help.

None of them could read or write, but I appointed them nurses, assuring them God would help them learn everything they needed to know. Through the day and for most of the night a seamstress worked to transform bed sheets into nurse's uniforms.

I found some cribs that were missing legs and hired men to break limbs from trees to make legs for the baby beds. Wire coat hangers, twisted in a criss-cross pattern, became the crib bottom to hold a mattress. A quick coat of white paint covered the not-so-new cribs.

Workers cut sheets of foam rubber for mattresses, which then were covered with oil cloth to keep them sanitary. Now we had seven cribs. Two babies would fit into each crib, one at each end. Everyone was excited. We were ready for our new babies.

With six new nurses in tow, I headed for the hospital on Saturday. We were greeted by a hospital spokesperson, who abruptly turned the excitement into heartbreak. "All fourteen babies died during the night," she announced. She went on to tell us that rain had come in through the window and all of the infants had been exposed.

Disbelief and horror overcame me momentarily. Then mustering a power greater than myself, I spoke up boldly. "We want some babies," I told the nurse. "We came for some babies and that is what we want! We're not going home empty-handed."

The nurse explained that they did have other babies, but they were very sick. They could not leave the hospital and most would probably die that very day. "Those are the ones I am to have," I quickly proclaimed. "We will take the sickly ones."

Once again the nurse refused and I headed straight for the doctor who was in with the babies. "What's wrong with this baby?" I demanded, pointing at one.

"Lady, these babies are all diseased and they are deformed in every way you can imagine," he answered. "Now move out of here, these babies are dying." He warned me not to touch anything as they were in a quarantined area due to certain skin diseases.

I backed off a little, but I did not move so far away that the doctor could not hear my firm demand. "Doctor, I am going to take all ten of these babies," I said. "Dead and dying are not the same. I know another physician."

"What is his name?" he demanded. "I know all the physicians in this hospital." When I began to share about the Great Physician, Jesus, the doctor fumed and walked away in disgust.

Before he left he gave me a rundown on the illnesses. There was the contagious skin disease. Another had no muscles around the eyes, causing them to droop. The baby would never be able to move his eyes, he said. Another had a bleeding scalp disease that would never heal. Another baby was born without a tailbone. The doctor said he would never crawl or walk. In addition, because he had a severe infestation of worms in his intestines, he probably could not live for very long.

I told the ladies to pick up all ten of the babies and take them out to the Jeep. I graciously thanked the doctor for his time and left the hospital.

Two days later reality sat in. Yes, the babies had a bright clean room, loving nurses and clean cribs, but they were very sick and required constant care. They had fevers, chills, convulsions and other things I could not even name.

"God, I know You told me to take these babies, now tell me what to do," I cried out. My mind was instantly drawn to the passage of scripture in 2 Chronicles 20, particularly verse 17: "Stand ye still, and see the salvation of the Lord."

The message of the entire passage challenged me and I passed the message on to the staff. I promptly organized the staff for regular praise and worship along with the children at the orphanage. One by one the children were lifted up to Jesus in prayer, while we loved and cared for them as best we could. Each day we continued to praise God for their healing.

One by one, God began to heal those babies. The one with the scalp problem grew hair where sores had once been. The baby with no eye muscles started moving his eyes (today his eyes are perfect). Over a period of two years God had completely healed nine of the ten children. Without ointments or medication, God completed the process as we praised and worshiped Him.

Little Girard — with no tailbone — was the last baby to experience a complete miracle of Jesus' healing power. Now three years old, he had been healed of intestinal worms, but he still could not walk. Hospital x-rays confirmed the diagnosis of a missing tailbone; nevertheless, the staff continued to praise God daily for Girard's complete restoration.

Each day one of the nurses would tie Girard to a chair in a sitting position. After every prayer time they would untie him to see if he was healed. One day during prayer time I glanced over to see Girard trying to remove the towels that had him bound. He was sliding down under the towels, moving under his own strength.

When I removed the towels, he dropped down to the floor. There was great rejoicing, as this was the first sign that the healing process had begun. They stopped tying Girard to the chair, but allowed him to lie on the floor where he would clap his hands and sing in French Creole, "Praise the Lord Eternal."

Two months passed, and one morning the workers discovered Girard on his knees holding to a chair. With each step of progress came great rejoicing. Another two months passed, and Girard was discovered standing, holding onto a chair. He would fall if he let go, but soon he was standing without any support from the chair. Before long he was taking long, stiff strides down the hallway. Today Girard is fully whole, horse-back riding, swimming and participating in all sports activities.

Another Miracle

The Social Welfare workers continued to bring babies to the orphanage. Each time, they would witness another miracle, and could scarcely believe what they saw. Many were convinced I had a brand-new form of voodoo. They could not bring themselves to believe these children, once given up for dead, were made whole by the healing power of Jesus. Truly, He is our Great Physician.

One day a worker from Social Welfare brought a very thin, sick little baby to me. Rachele had been abandoned at the hospital at the age of four months. Since the first day she came to us she has heard the name of Jesus and how much He loves her, and that He is her doctor. All my children hear that Jesus loves them from the time they arrive at the orphanage.

Some children's faith grows more rapidly than others. From the beginning this little girl was a very special person, and her faith just blossomed as she grew. I have seen her walk over to other children who were sick and lay hands on them and say, "Jesus, heal this baby," and then walk away, confident that Jesus would do just that.

When Rachele was about four years old, I had a very sick baby in the nursery. Little eight-month-old Sammy had a very high fever complicated by convulsions. No matter what we did, we could not bring the fever down. His eyes were set, his back arched, and he was trembling from head to toe. I ran down the long hallway to get an ice pack for him.

On the way to the kitchen I saw Rachele sitting on the floor playing with a rag doll that some Americans had given her. "Run to little Samuel quickly and pray for him — he is real sick," I said. She immediately dropped her doll on the floor and ran off to the nursery. She knew exactly the place where Samuel's crib was located. Running up to the crib, she stuck her little arm through the bars of the crib and said in Creole, "Jesus, touch Samuel, please. Thank You!" Then she took off down the hall to play with her doll again.

At this point I was just coming around the corner of the kitchen with the ice in my hand. She stopped me and looked directly in my face with her big, brown, gleaming eyes and said, "Mama, you don't need that ice. Jesus touched Samuel."

I stuttered for a minute, then said, "Okay, Honey — now go on outside and play." But she kept insisting that Jesus had finished with Samuel. I said, "Okay — I heard you. Now go play outside."

Rachele just stood there looking at that ice bag in my hand. Finally I laid the bag of ice on top of a nearby refrigerator, and she ran down the hall and outside. When I heard the screen door slam I retrieved my ice pack and ran as fast as I could to Samuel's corner of the nursery. Looking into his crib, I got the shock of my life. He was lying there kicking and cooing like any healthy baby. I touched him and there was no fever. As my eyes nearly popped out of my head and my mouth dropped open, the ice pack fell to the floor scattering ice everywhere. I fell to my knees and said, "Oh, God, You have given Samuel a miracle! Thank You! Please, Lord, I need what Rachele has — please give me that kind of faith."

He sent His Word to heal our diseases. (Psalm 107:20). This is what is taught to all of our children from their early beginnings. We had taught little Rachele from the time she was a crib baby that Jesus is the Great Physician, and she believed it.

I went after God with a renewed spirit and prayed differently from that time on — knowing that God will do exactly as He promises in His Word when we trust Him. How humbling to have a four-year-old make known to me that the very thing I was teaching the children, I was lacking in my own life.

5

Blended Family

A father of the fatherless, a defender of widows.... God sets the solitary in families; He brings out those who are bound into prosperity....

Psalm 68:5-6

It takes a lot of hard work and strong faith in God for an American or Canadian couple to make it through the process of adopting one or more of our CHO children. Phil and Carla's story is a typical example. This couple had tried for more than a year — through several different agencies — to adopt an American special needs or biracial child. But in each case, one obstacle after another resulted in disappointment.

Finally they called a couple they heard about who had adopted children from Haiti, and that couple referred them to me. When I told them we require prospective parents to visit the orphanage in person and seek God's guidance as to which child they should adopt, Phil and Carla decided to come to Haiti for Christmas that year.

After their arrival they spent the next day and a half wandering in and out of the infants' room. Then Phil met Timothé, a twelve-year-old boy in the orphanage. "Would you adopt me?" he asked. "Or are you just here for a baby?" Nothing in his life had prepared Phil to answer such a question.

"Well," Phil gulped, "you pray, and I will pray. I know that God will give us the same answer." When Phil told Carla they might need to rethink their adoption plan, her readiness to reconsider something they had agreed to years earlier surprised him. Then he found out why. A twelve-year-old girl named Dina had sent an envoy to ask Carla the same question. So the couple came to me to ask about adopting older children instead of infants.

Dina had four brothers and sisters — Nancy, 14; Ralph, 7; Marly, 6; and Jeff, 5. However, since these five children had no papers, they were not available for adoption. After their father had died and their mother became ill, the Haitian Ministry of Social Welfare placed them at CHO but the mother had not formally relinquished custody.

I sent a courier to find the woman to see if she would sign relinquishment papers, as Phil and Carla wanted these five siblings, and Timothé too. The courier returned with the message that the woman had moved and left no forwarding address. Phil and Carla returned to Kentucky not knowing whether they would ever find the birth mother. They could only pray earnestly as I had advised them to — that God would somehow release all six of these children and make them a family. It looked impossible, but I believed it would happen.

A week later I called them with good news: we had found the siblings' mother. Pastor Luc Deratus, the Haitian vice-president of CHO who helps us with adoptions, had talked with her and she had agreed to sign relinquishment papers. But when Paul contacted the Department of Social Services in Kentucky, he learned some bad news. He and Carla would be required to post a $10,000 bond for each child, except in the case of biological siblings. Also, they could apply for the five siblings, or for Timothé, but not for all six at the same time. They decided to apply for the five first, believing God would provide a way for Timothé to join them later on. A new social worker was assigned to them, and they began all over again to collect documents for their homestudy program.

The new social worker tried to discourage them from moving ahead with a Haitian adoption, hoping to keep them from being disappointed. Then when he discovered Phil and Carla lived in a one-bedroom apartment, he said he would not finish the homestudy until they bought a house big enough for a family of seven. They made three offers on a house, only to be refused by the seller, then a mortgage company, and then the seller again. Next, Pastor Luc reported that the children's birth mother had changed her mind and would not sign the relinquishment papers after all, and their social worker informed Phil and Carla their homestudy would be closed unless they found a house.

Amazingly, these prospective parents refused to give up. They wrote to several of their state legislators and to the governor about getting a law changed to simplify the process for pursuing foreign adoptions. I reminded them, "The king's heart is in the hands of the Lord," (Proverbs 21:1), and Carla made this verse into a poster and put it on their refrigerator. They continued to pray.

One legislator — a Christian who happened to chair the very committee with the power to change the law — took a particular interest in their situation. When he invited Phil and Carla to the capitol to speak before his committee, they borrowed some of their friends' adopted children and made the two-hour drive. A gray-suited Social Services official talked about policy; Phil and Carla talked about human lives — children who wanted to be a family.

They talked about the five siblings who wanted to stay together, and Timothé, who had been abandoned at the Port-au-Prince public hospital at birth. There was no information about his birth parents. His name, Timothé Paul, had been given not by his mother, but by me. I chose to name him Timothé, and he had been named Paul because the mayor of Port-au-Prince at the time of the boy's birth had been a man named Franck Paul. According to Haitian tradition, foundlings receive the name of the mayor.

The legislative committee gave Social Services one month to return with information to support their position. On September 3, 1993, Carla returned to the capitol and learned that the "king" had had a change of heart! The state agreed to reword their policy in order to permit application for more than one child at a time. September 3 is Timothé's birthday. How beautiful, how heartwarming is God's sense of humor!

About this time Pastor Luc blessed Phil and Carla with news of God's intervention in Haiti. The children's mother had come to him and agreed to sign relinquishment papers after all, and he planned to take her to the tribunal within the week.

The following month Phil and Carla found a house and got approval on a loan. They called their social worker with this report, only to be reminded of the money they would need to post in bonds. He also told them they must have medical histories, birth certificates or official abandonment papers, and passports and visas for each of the children. At about the same time word came that the Haitian government would allow them to adopt only three of the children — not six. The end of the year was fast approaching, and Pastor Luc, who had been working to get the needed documents for the children, planned to leave Haiti on December 28 for a three-month stay in the U.S.

It appeared an evil conspiracy was intent on thwarting Phil and Carla's dream of having a family of six children. Refusing to give up, they decided to once again travel to Haiti for Christmas to work on the problems.

Pastor Luc took them to meet with the government worker handling the adoption, but she only confirmed what they had been told: Haitian policy limited them to adopting only three children. When pressed, the worker said they could apply for the other two siblings in two or three years. But they would never be permitted to adopt Timothé. Phil and Carla insisted on speaking with the Director of Social Welfare, who had the authority to make an exception. He would only be available at 2:00 that afternoon.

This determined pair camped outside his office until he finally appeared, invited them into his office, and was willing to talk with them. But he simply restated the existing policy: it was impossible for them to adopt six children at once. They prayed. He agreed to let them have three first, then three months later allow them to apply for two more. But he would not allow Timothé to be adopted. This was an improvement, but it wasn't good enough for them. They remained seated, continuing to pray. "I have told you my decision," he said. "Why aren't you leaving?"

"What about Timothé?" Carla pleaded. "He has begun to call us 'Mama' and 'Papa' now — how can we tell him that we must leave him behind?"

"I told you you could have five children," he warned, becoming annoyed. "Be happy with that." Obviously the Director expected them to leave, but they stayed in their chairs and prayed. A law in Kentucky had been changed for Timothé; they weren't giving up now. Finally the Director gave in and nodded "yes." He would allow them to adopt all six; first three, then two, then Timothé. Tears filled Phil's eyes as he left that government building. And they would fill with tears again before their week in Haiti ended.

I sent a translator with Phil and Carla, along with the older siblings, to talk with the mother about the needed birth certificates, and to ask about a death certificate for the husband. It was an unforgettable meeting. She explained why she had wavered about signing the relinquishment papers: she had heard that Americans let children go to nightclubs and stay out late at night. Also, Social Welfare had told her the five children would be split up. Had she been assured these things wouldn't happen — and had she met Phil and Carla face to face — she would have signed the papers earlier. But unfortunately, she had none of the documents they needed so badly.

The mother asked this young couple to make several promises to her: That they would enroll the children in school, that the girls would get married when they grew up, and that they would treat the children as their own flesh and blood. They promised.

"Today I will tell you what no one else can tell you," she said at last. "These children are your children. Today I give you my children."

Phil and Carla told her good-bye, and knew they would never forget her. But because they couldn't get the needed documents, they went back to the States alone. A few days later, word came that the mother had died.

In March, bad news came from Louisville and from Haiti. Kentucky had approved their homestudy, but without birth certificates the Immigration and Naturalization Service could not process the visa applications. INS also informed them that U.S. law prohibits immigration of an adopted child older than sixteen years. Nancy's sixteenth birthday was just one month away.

Our CHO attorney then called to say that Haiti also had a policy of not allowing the adoption of a sixteen-year-old, and until Phil could supply the needed documents translated into French and stamped by the Haitian Consulate, he could not approach the tribunal. Time was running out. Phil promised he would be back in Haiti in one week with the necessary papers.

Sure enough, the last pages of translations arrived a few days later, and Phil had them notarized and took them to the Haitian Consulate in Chicago to obtain the official stamp. Within a short time he was on his way to Haiti, documents in hand. While on the plane Paul remembered something I had said to him months earlier: "God is the God of 11:59."

What followed during his time in Haiti was a maze of confusion. Phil felt like a ping-pong ball being bounced back and forth between Haitian and U.S.

bureaucratic obstacles. As quickly as one requirement was met, he learned of one or two others. In addition to all the documents he had already gathered, he had to return to the U.S. to request a fingerprint check on himself and Carla by the Federal Bureau of Investigation, and to get the INS to issue Form I-600 so the U.S. Consulate in Haiti would grant visas to the children.

Meanwhile, Pastor Luc was able to get passports for only three of the six children. Then I learned that the embargo against Haiti was being stepped up and I feared that all flights would be cancelled indefinitely. "The door is closing," I told Paul, calling him at work. "You must come to Haiti at once or you may not be able to the get the kids out."

Carla decided to come to Haiti immediately, while Phil stayed in the U.S. to try to obtain the final clearances needed to get the children's visas issued. At last, events began moving in their favor. Carla convinced the Haitian authorities to release all six children for adoption at the same time, and they issued passports for all of them. Phil was able to get everything he needed from the FBI and the INS, and join Carla in Haiti. Every day God gave them a miracle, and they prayed for the next day's needed miracle.

On the first day they got visa photos for all the children; on the second day they completed medical exams; on the third day the boys' passports arrived. On the fourth day they applied for all the children's visas, and on the fifth day the visas were issued. That night Carla called the airline to reconfirm their departure for the next day. Phil and Carla's reservations were confirmed, but for some mysterious reason the children's reservations had been canceled. They determined to get to the airport early the next day to work out the problem.

Sure enough, the flight was overbooked, but God gave them favor and the airline agent reinstated the reservations. They passed through all the checkpoints and made it to the plane at last. Only after they were watching Port-au-Prince disappear in the mists below could they relax and exclaim, "Thank You, Lord!"

The first fifteen minutes in Miami with their six children was worth the years of difficulties and waiting for Phil and Carla. The kids were so excited by escalators, moving walkways, warm water at hand basins, lavatory hand dryers and drinking fountains that Paul's face hurt from smiling so much. The older kids pulled their shirts over their heads to protect themselves from the chill of air-conditioning, and they all spoke to each other in the fastest Creole Phil and Carla had ever heard.

Jesus replaced their tears of desperation and sighs of disappointment with the sparkle of ebony eyes and the happy sounds of childhood laughter. He had done it, just as I always said He would.

At the time of this writing CHO has completed 127 adoptions to place our children in homes in the U.S. and in Canada. And every story of adoption is full of miracles, just as Phil and Carla's story is.

6

Jean Daniel — Our Special Baby

But he said to me, "My grace is sufficient for you, for my power is made perfect in weakness." Therefore I will boast all the more gladly about my weaknesses, so that Christ's power may rest on me.

2 Corinthians 12:9 NIV

In November and December of 1985, seven babies arrived at the CHO orphanage, bringing the total to forty-three children living on our compound in Mariani. One boy died of dehydration, but the others all became healthy and strong.

A Social Welfare worker had told me on the phone that one of the seven had very serious problems, but she provided no details. I assured her we would take the baby no matter what his problems were and care for him as best we could. That special baby was Jean Daniel Marc.

A group of thirty-five Americans happened to be at the orphanage on a work trip when the Social Welfare workers brought Jean Daniel to us the day after Thanksgiving. We fell in love with him; everyone was excited and happy to have this wonderful new addition to the family. He truly was a Thanksgiving gift to us.

The workers were quite surprised at how different Jean (pronounced like "John") Daniel was from all the other babies who had come to us over the years. He was born with deformed arms and legs. We don't know who had cared for him during the first three months of his life, but whoever kept him had decided for some reason to abandon him at the University Hospital in Port-au-Prince — perhaps because of his deformities. For most Haitians, a child born with such problems is considered to be an evil omen.

The first thing the American group did was to anoint him with oil and pray for him. He was very thin and weak. He seldom cried, but his eyes were full of fear, as if he had been through some frightening experience. The doctor in the group gave him a good checking over, and found that he was badly dehydrated. In fact, the doctor said if Jean Daniel had not come to us when he did, he probably would not have lived more than another day or two. At three months old, he weighed just six pounds, nine ounces!

We gave him his own crib, and since the visitors had just brought a lot of new baby clothes, we were able to keep him well dressed. As we prayed often for him, fed him well, and held him during most of his waking hours, he grew rapidly in both weight and strength. His left arm functioned well and was strong, but the hand on that arm was not fully formed. His right forearm, hand and fingers were not completely developed. His legs were small and deformed, and his feet were disfigured. Without a miracle, Jean Daniel would never be able to walk.

We never underestimate the power of prayers, both ours and the children's. Twice daily we have our "Baby Prayer Time," when we bring all the children into a central room to sing praise songs, recite Bible verses, and pray for one another and for all who work at the orphanage. As we included Jean Daniel in these prayer times, the look of fear in his eyes faded, and his delightful personality began to shine.

Upon returning to the U.S., a member of the American group found out about a hospital in Texas where doctors and therapists help children who have problems like Jean Daniel's. They perform needed surgery, attaching artificial limbs and providing therapy so crippled children can live relatively normal lives. At this hospital, supported entirely by grants and trust funds, patients are never charged for services. There is not even a billing department; financial eligibility requirements do not exist.

But there was a problem. Because of the enormous demand for their services, the hospital charter states that only children who reside in Texas can be accepted as patients. Exceptions are made — and they are rare — only if a particular case has special merit for research and study purposes.

My friends in Texas, who are long-time prayer partners, visited the hospital's social director and explained the situation. They gave her photographs of Jean Daniel, along with copies of the limited medical records we had, which they had had translated from French to English. The woman responded warmly and gave the two a personal tour of the hospital. When the Board of Surgeons read the dossier and saw photos of Jean Daniel's severe congenital deformities of the skeletal system, they agreed to admit him as a teaching case. Thus began a series of miracles we would see God perform in Jean Daniel's life.

In the months which followed, the Lord helped the

two prayer partners surmount one obstacle after another to obtain paperwork the hospital and the immigration authorities required so that we could take the next step. Soon one of them was on a plane bound for Haiti to bring ten-month-old Jean Daniel back to Texas with her. God gave favor with all the Haitian and U.S. authorities involved, so we accomplished in a few days what normally would take many months.

The other prayer partner met her friend at the airport with a stroller to take the baby home with her, as she had agreed to be his temporary conservator while he was in Texas for treatment. Since she is a registered nurse, a mother, and a prayer warrior, she was well qualified to care for this very special little boy. Also, she had been in the group of visitors at the orphanage the day Jean Daniel first arrived.

Friends of CHO volunteered legal services, provided translation for the documents involved in Jean Daniel's case, and donated various items needed for his care. Others donated funds to cover such costs as his passport, photos, medical evaluations, airfare and other related expenses. Dozens of people were praying for the entire situation, and God's answers to those prayers were continually evident in the events surrounding young Jean Daniel's life. All of us strongly believed that God would use this little boy as a channel to minister to people both in the United States and in Haiti.

Every twelve months we had to request permission from the INS for Jean Daniel to remain in the United States for the care he required, because his problems could not be solved in a short period of time. Each time the request was granted.

Our precious Jean Daniel underwent multiple

surgeries, followed by laborious and often painful therapy sessions. After the first surgery to remove his right foot, he was fitted with a prosthesis so he was able to stand by himself when he was two-and-a-half years old. Later the other leg had to be amputated and fitted with a prosthesis, and as he grew these devices had to be resized and replaced. He cooperated with the therapists and worked very hard to learn to walk and to do as much as possible in spite of his limitations. All the hospital workers were smitten by his engaging smile, his positive attitude, and his witty personality.

Jean Daniel's problems were extremely complex, requiring a very sophisticated team approach to manage them and make his body as functional as possible. The doctors who attended him recognized that he was an extremely bright and articulate child, so they continued working to increase his mobility and quality of life. During this time all his living expenses were being met through contributions to CHO. We assured the U.S. immigration officials that Jean Daniel would never become a burden to the welfare system.

After his first year in Texas, a different couple took over Jean Daniel's care, and they began praying God would allow them to adopt him. In April of 1990 I had the joy of signing the legal adoption papers, and Jean Daniel officially became the son of this dear couple who already had two other children. The stimulation of having siblings has helped Jean Daniel adjust well to being around other children, and the church family he is a part of love and accept him. When I visited him in Texas I was thrilled to see that he is so well-adjusted.

All the surgeries were focused on helping him to be able to walk, which he finally was able to do with his prosthetics. But little could be done about the fact that he has no hands. His only mobile finger is a thumb at the end of his left arm, and on that arm he has a little finger that is only partially mobile. That is enough to allow him to hold things, and there is almost nothing he needs to do which he cannot manage.

He has learned to feed and dress himself. He can throw a basketball by holding it between his arms, and he can write. He simply does not let his disabilities prevent him from doing what he wants to do. Jean Daniel is a talented and resourceful problem solver, even without equipment to help him. "Sometimes having him to solve problems on his own is better therapy," remarked one of his physical therapists.

"He just amazes me," his mother says. "He makes me feel that you can never say you can't do something when you look at your own two hands."

Today he is a young teenager with lots of friends, doing well in school, and greatly loved by his family. Thanks be to our Lord Jesus, to whom Jean Daniel was no "pro-choice" throw-away child. His is a precious life, and we praise God for the miracles He has done for this exceptional child. In the future I expect to hear reports of him doing mighty exploits for God.

7

Verdy Gerad Lives Evermore

> **I tell you the truth, unless a kernel of wheat falls to the ground and dies, it remains only a single seed. But if it dies, it produces many seeds.**
>
> **John 12:24 NIV**

Early in February of 1989, four new babies arrived at Christian Haitian Outreach. Like so many of our babies they had been abandoned. We didn't know who their parents were, how old they were, or why they were left. These are questions to which only God has answers.

All four babies arrived sick and very weak from severe malnutrition, each of them weighing under three pounds. They bore signs of neglect — swollen and bulging eyes, and tightly drawn skin. All four were approximately two to three months old, as best we could estimate.

My faith is always enlarged by great measure as I watch the hand of God at work with my infants. Many sick babies come here, and God miraculously touches them, heals them and restores them to perfect health within weeks, days and even hours.

This time, after a few days with our new babies, we began to see measurable changes within Marylude, Jonathan, and JoNeil, as they increased in strength. But Verdy was another story.

Verdy graced the world with a perfect rosebud mouth, a full head of long, tightly curled hair, and large, round brown eyes. Despite his attractive countenance, Verdy carried a deep and pervasive sadness or despair that we could see in his eyes. He shared no smiles with us, and he never seemed to bond to any of the nurses or helpers who shared in his daily care. Though he was a tiny infant, his face was like the face of an older person who had given up on life.

This look has become all too familiar to me in Haiti. Some of these children enter the world with no determination to live and grow. This attitude is understandable, because many of them have barely clung to life while being almost starved to death inside their pregnant mothers. Life in the outside world has proven no better. For them, life equals pain.

These children know the suffering life can hold on this earth, even before they have words to articulate it. They have experienced it vicariously in their mother's womb, and learned it by sharing their mother's pain and despair.

Verdy had great difficulty eating. He had been so undernourished from the start that his stomach was not capable of taking in much food at a time. We fed him every hour, around the clock, using a tiny eyedropper, gently placing drops of baby formula in his mouth and waiting for the drops to roll back down his slender throat. His stomach often rejected it and he would spit up the milk. We would wait another hour, then start the painstaking but essential process all over again.

There were times when we felt like Verdy was making progress and getting healthier. We thought there was a spark of interest in living which was taking hold in him. But Verdy did not gain any weight. By the end of his ninth day with us, his tiny body began to convulse as one of the nurses was feeding him.

This happened shortly before five o'clock in the afternoon, as we gathered the children for prayer time. I carried Verdy into the room and sat on a metal folding chair, calling the children to gather around me.

The smallest of them, some not even two years old, formed an inner half-circle and pressed in to lay their little hands on their tiny, sick brother. The older children were right behind them with many of their hands touching the shoulders of the tots whose hands rested on Verdy. My oldest children formed a third half-circle, their hands extended toward Verdy, and all the children prayed earnestly for this precious new baby.

God so graciously honors the simple and sincere prayers of my little ones here. Many miraculous healings have taken place during this prayer time or as a result of the prayers prayed during that time. But as we prayed for Verdy that day, his little body continued to tremble in my hands. It was not a violent shaking, but Verdy's health was precarious, and he had no extra energy to spend. His condition was not to be taken lightly, and we knew it.

Prayer time was over at about 5:30 p.m., and the children were dismissed for supper. I took Verdy to the office with me, holding him as securely as I could, but his tiny little body continued to tremble. I called one of our drivers to pull the bus up to the front of the orphanage as I wrapped Verdy up for his journey to the Seventh Day Adventist Hospital. I was so distressed that I didn't even think to bring additional clothes for Verdy, not even a diaper. We had not a moment to delay.

Verdy's listless body lay limp and quiet in my arms as our bus bounced down the rocky, crowded Carrefour Road. I recalled the countless times God had marvelously saved my children against the highest of odds. Many babies whom doctors told me would not live now were healthy and living in safe homes with loving families. As I held this little one I asked the Lord to once again show me His miraculous healing power, to touch my Verdy and make him whole.

At about 6:30 p.m. we arrived at the hospital. Taking a quick glance at Verdy, the nurses recognized the seriousness of his condition and ushered us right into the emergency room. They placed Verdy carefully on the examining table.

The doctor was focused on a particularly bloody emergency case, so he did not notice us as we entered the room. A twelve-year-old girl had fallen on a coke bottle, causing it to break and splinter. Parts of the shattered bottle were lodged in her right hand, and he had no local anaesthetic to dull the girl's pain and ease the procedure. She cried out in a continual high-pitched shriek. Her parents held her down while the doctor removed the slivers and shards of glass from her hand.

We waited for almost an hour for the doctor, and all during this time Verdy's body convulsed. Just as the doctor finished bandaging the other child's wounds, Verdy's body stopped quivering, and he quietly slipped into eternity.

In the seventeen years I had served the Lord in Haiti, only one other baby placed in my care had died.

Verdy was the second little boy the Lord chose to take home. I really didn't think this baby would die, so I was not fully prepared for it. The deep sense of loss and the sudden nature of Verdy's death made it difficult for me to think clearly and to gain God's perspective.

We were not certain how best to proceed from there. The doctor told us we could take the baby to the General Hospital and just walk away, saving us the trouble of disposing of the body. As he observed the expressions on our faces, however, he offered another alternative — we could call a funeral home. My nurses made several phone calls to surrounding funeral homes, only to find out they would charge more than $500 to pick up the baby and prepare him for burial. That was impossible for us financially.

Just then the driver spoke up and said, "Mom, I'll go do something." He knew a young man who had just opened a funeral parlor not far from us on Carrefour Road. His friend picked up our little Verdy's body and placed him in a tub with chipped ice around him for overnight preservation.

Sometimes we do not fully understand God's plan, but this time the wisdom of God was quickly unveiled and revealed to us. As I began to make burial preparations for Verdy, I was reminded also of a word which God had given me a few days before, through a worker from Ohio who had come to help us that week. As she prayed for Verdy, the Lord gave her a middle name for him: Gerad. She felt that in giving Verdy a new name, God was giving him the promise of a long life, because Gerad means "long life. "

But, how could Verdy have a long life now? In the coming days I would see that God had not only given

Verdy Gerad a new and everlasting life, but He would use his short earthly life to bring the message of eternal life to others.

The painful process of making burial preparations for Verdy filled much of the next day for me. In Haiti, burials for the poor must be taken care of quickly because embalming is too costly. The heat in Haiti and the rampant disease require the dead be buried as quickly as possible. Most burials among the poor in Haiti therefore take place the very same day a person dies.

One of the carpenters who was working on our new school immediately stopped what he was doing and began making a casket for Verdy Gerad. I stopped at the tribunal to pay the required twenty-five-dollar fee to obtain permission to bury the baby in the cemetery. I then paid the customary twenty-five dollars to have a cemetery employee dig the hole for the grave. Finally, I sorted through some new clothing which had just been donated to find suitable clothes in which to bury our precious child.

We are often asked to provide burial clothes in Haiti, because many times people in the community have no means to bury their dead and no clothing in which to bury them. Many people lose their children to disease or malnutrition. One out of five children born in Haiti dies before the age of five. Parents often turn to me for help with burial needs when their child dies — how can I refuse at such a critical and difficult time in their lives?

We were able to find an attractive little outfit for Verdy and a small pillow and soft blanket to place in his casket. The funeral was scheduled for four o'clock in the afternoon at the cemetery. We did not bring the baby to the church, nor let the other children at the orphanage know what had happened.

A small group of us gathered at the graveside, very heavy in heart. The group was mostly workers who had shared in Verdy's care for the short time he had on earth, and one or two visitors. It was an especially difficult time for the missionary nurse who so often had held Verdy rocking him tenderly in her arms throughout the days and into the nights.

We began to sing songs of praise to our Lord, which helped us to release all the perplexing questions in our minds and the heaviness in our hearts. As we lifted up our praises to the Lord, He graciously lifted up our spirits.

While we stood around the casket at the cemetery, a crowd began to gather. Because there is so little to do there, it is easy to attract a crowd in Haiti. I am sure the Lord used our simple choruses of praise and worship to draw the people to us.

As I stood before the curious spectators, the Spirit of the Lord came upon me. I knew He wanted me to take advantage of this opportunity to share Jesus with those who were filled with wonder at what these Americans were doing. Shifting my focus from Verdy and my staff to these people the Lord had brought before us, I began to direct my words toward them.

"This precious newborn baby went to be with Jesus," I began. "He went to be with Jesus because he is pure and innocent — he is sinless. He is therefore perfect before God. His time on this earth was brief; he knew nothing about right or wrong; he knew nothing about sin.

"However, you have been on earth long enough to know right from wrong. Each of you has made the choice to do many things which are right and many things which are wrong. You all have knowledge of sin and an awareness of sin in your own lives. You have most likely paid some kind of price for the wrongs you have done. You have sensed your wrongs through guilt and shame, or through a nudging in your conscience.

"But I tell you today that there is a Savior, and His name is Jesus. He is the Son of God and the Son of Man. He came to provide forgiveness for all who have sinned and fallen short of the glory of God. His invitation extends to every one of us, because if we are honest we will admit that we've done wrong. We know that we need a Savior.

"Now is the time to ask for forgiveness, because we all, like this tiny baby, are headed for the grave. The man who dug this grave for little Verdy will someday have a grave dug for him. It may be soon, or it may be later. But that day will certainly come for each of us. Someday we will be placed down into a deep hole, just as this baby is being placed in this hole today.

"If we have a right relationship with God, our destiny is assured; we know that we are going to a better place — a place where He dwells, a place He has prepared for us. Today, if you choose Him, you can have the assurance that the Lord is preparing a place for you. The choice is in your hands — just as Moses said to the Israelites, 'I set before you life and death. Choose life.' You can make the choice today. "

Six individuals accepted Jesus as their Savior that day! I was so delighted. The gravedigger was so convicted by the Holy Spirit that he dropped to his knees right there on the rocks and asked us to pray for him to be saved. We spoke the sinner's prayer, and the six repeated it after us. We invited the six to come to the church to receive literature and a Bible. We told them when we have Bible study at the church and invited them to attend.

The man who dug the grave for Verdy rushed back from the cemetery to our compound to receive his Bible, and we found him waiting for us when we arrived there an hour later. The glory of the Lord shone brightly on his face as we placed a Bible in his hands. This was for us as it is written in Psalms, "You turned my wailing into dancing; you removed my sackcloth and clothed me with joy" (Psalm 30:11 NIV). The Lord turned something which was very sad for us into something very glorious. There in the cemetery, a place for the dead, God had wrought a rich work of new life.

The short life of Verdy Gerad was a rich treasure for the Kingdom of God, for his name is written in the Lamb's Book of Life. Because this baby's earthly life fell to the ground like a seed, it produced a harvest of souls, bringing six individuals into fellowship with our Lord Jesus. He has left behind a legacy of everlasting life through those whose lives he touched. Praise be to God.

8
Two, Three, Then Four

The Twins

> **When the child grew older, she took him to Pharaoh's daughter and he became her son. She named him Moses, saying, "I drew him out of the water."**
>
> **Exodus 2:10 NIV**

One of the greatest joys we have at CHO is uniting needy young children with caring families through adoption. In His divine grace, God has often taken children with needs which cannot be met here in Haiti, and brought them together with couples in whose hearts He has placed a burden for the kind of ministry opportunity which only a child can provide. How beautiful it is to watch God bring these children and adults together through adoption, and how joyous it is for everyone involved.

About ten years ago twin babies were found in a distressed area of Port-au-Prince and brought to our compound by a doctor. He estimated the twins were about six weeks old, and he told us as helpless as they were, they would not have survived in the conditions where they had been found. He asked if I would take them. Of course I said yes.

It was more difficult than you could imagine to just clean them up and get all the mud and grime off of these two babies, one boy and one girl. There was axle grease and awful filth stuck to them so tenaciously that we had to repeatedly apply warm oil, then soap, finally rinsing them with warm water to get them cleaned up. We soon discovered two gorgeous little babies, gifts from God to us. They were both undernourished of course, but in a short time our care and the Lord's help brought them to good health and full strength.

These two beautiful children were adopted by precious friends of mine in New Jersey. When the twins were five years old, Brent and Glenda gave them piano lessons and discovered they had a little genius on their hands — the little boy was going to be a child prodigy for sure.

The little girl plays beautifully also, but the boy has a special gift from the Lord. He is ten years old now. He has been playing for five years, and is taking music lessons at Radio City Music Hall in New York City. He is in line to study music at the Julliard School of Music. Can you imagine, going from the desolation of Haiti to the Julliard School of Music in New York? That is truly a miracle that only God could perform.

God continues to bless the children who come to us. He moves them out of Haiti by adoption and into wonderful homes with Christian families, who are willing to give them all the love they need and every opportunity to learn and grow. Some of our adopted children are now in the Unites States, and some are in Canada. We praise the Lord for every one who has been placed, because they all seem to be with a family that is exactly right for them.

We continue to pray for the children we have who would like to be adopted. I believe God will bless each one of these children, whether they ever get out of Haiti, or whether they remain and learn to give of themselves in service to the Lord.

The Triplets

Often we have no advance warning before children are brought to us. One day three babies arrived — triplets! Just six months old, they were very small. First there was Maggie, who was tiny, and had breathing problems. She was such a fighter, and how she held onto life. Her two sisters Marjorie and Myriame were healthier than she.

Maggie was adopted quickly, but it was a constant struggle for Don and Ellen, her new parents, to keep her alive at first. After she grew healthy and strong, Don and Ellen had a different struggle on their hands — keeping up with the fast-moving Maggie. She progressed to the point where no one would have guessed that she was a very sick baby when she came to our orphanage.

During the next four years, Don and Ellen spoke to little Maggie about her other triplet sisters, Marjorie and Myriame. They would show her pictures of them, and together they would pray for them.

From the time they received Maggie and had to leave her two sisters behind in Haiti, my friends believed that someday the three sisters would be together again in their household in the United States. For the next four years, their prayers went up and their efforts went forth.

Many hindrances prevented their adopting the remaining two sisters. Ellen approached each step toward the hoped-for adoption with prayer, hoping the political difficulties in Haiti would not close the doors on her dream. God blessed them with helpful people in Florida, Illinois, Tennessee, and Washington, D.C., whose efforts brought them closer to adopting Marjorie and Myriame. Phone calls were made to Florida and to Haiti every day, working through problems and ironing out details.

As the political turmoil in Haiti intensified, there was talk of a possible United States invasion of the island. I was in frequent contact with Don and Ellen, and one week I got news that air traffic was scheduled to cease between the two countries the following Friday. I knew in my spirit that time was running out and the two girls must be gotten out quickly.

Ellen came to Haiti immediately. But there was a catch — she would have only one day to finalize all that needed to be done in Haiti and bring the girls out. Considering the Haitian bureaucracy, this seemed impossible. Still, Ellen flew to Port-au-Prince on a Tuesday. Upon arriving she found that all the necessary papers were completed and ready for her to pick up at the United States Embassy.

Ellen and the two girls left Haiti on Wednesday — *on schedule*. All flights to and from Haiti ceased two days later. Clearly, the circumstances enabling her to get the girls out in that time window did not happen by themselves — it was the Lord Who brought them together and enabled Ellen to leave for the United States with the girls that day. Maggie, Marjorie, and Myriame were finally united, just in time to celebrate their fifth birthday together.

All three girls began preschool classes together in order to prepare them for kindergarten the following year. These three girls are so alike, and yet they are such distinct individuals. They play together, singing, dancing, and yes, even fighting as siblings typically do. Don and Ellen completed the legalities for adopting Marjorie and Myriame on December 27, 1994.

With the triplets, as with so many other children before and since, it was God's blessing and favor and many answers to prayer resulting in their being able to celebrate birthdays and Christmases together in a better place, with new parents who love them dearly.

By the time Don and Ellen had nine children in their family, construction began on enlarging their home. The project was made possible through donations from many people, both churches and individuals, in Iowa and Minnesota.

Volunteer workers came from all over a three-state area to build an addition over Don and Ellen's garage, giving them a large closet, a bedroom, and an office. The workers installed a new roof, and a great deal of refurbishing was done in their basement and living areas. Many people donated large quantities of food.

By the end of 1994 this amazing couple was raising a family of thirteen children, nine of whom we had placed with them from our orphanage in Haiti.

And Then There Were Four

In the last half of 1994, extraordinary things began to happen at CHO. Social workers brought four newborn babies to us in less than three weeks. The first one was found on the ground on a street in the downtown area of Port-au-Prince by missionaries who took him to the Social Welfare Department. They estimated he was no more than two days old at that time.

Virginia, our administrator in Haiti, named him Moses, because the story of how he was found reminded her of how Moses was found by Pharaoh's daughter by the Nile. Once again it was Don and Ellen to the rescue. From the United States they flew their eldest daughter to Miami to meet with one of our visiting nurses who was leaving Haiti just in time to bring baby Moses out.

With her knowledge of nursing, this volunteer worker knew exactly how to handle such a tiny, sick newborn, with his serious respiratory problems and his persistent diarrhea. We could never have given little Moses the proper care his condition required, so we were blessed to get him out for treatment.

Ellen took him to medical specialists willing to donate their services, and Moses received treatment for his breathing problems and overcame them. A formula change and a five-day course of antibiotics cleared his digestive condition. Moses had come out of Haiti on a medical visa, but Ellen and Don couldn't bring themselves to send him back, so they adopted him. They renamed this one Noah, as he had found favor in the sight of God. And they truly feel blessed by God to have him. Today Noah is perfectly healthy. He is alert, cute, and well behaved.

God truly has been good to Noah, and to the parents who feel humbled at the responsibilities bestowed upon them in the form of these dear children. How we thank God for such friends who open their hearts and their homes to Haiti's abandoned children.

9

Dr. Jean Franco Jean Louis

The king's heart is in the hand of the LORD; he directs it like a watercourse wherever he pleases.

Proverbs 21:1 NIV

Five years after I opened the orphanage, someone brought a child named Franco to our gate and told us he would like for the boy to be able to attend my school. Franco was very thin, but he had a beautiful smile, big, deep eyes, and nice brown skin. He was a very pleasant and likable little fellow.

I took him in and he started school in the second grade, though he was eleven years old. After he had been with us for about three months, I was with Franco on the playground one day when he said to me, "Mom, someday I am going to be a doctor." "Yes, you are," I told him, "and I am going to help you become a doctor." He became like my own son, and we were very close.

He really enjoyed the daily prayer we had at the orphanage from 7:30-8:00 a.m., before classes began. He would always bring his report card and show it to me. Of course I could not read it, because it was in French, but I would always make a big fuss about it anyway, saying, "How nice! You are really on your way to becoming a doctor; you are making a good start."

He did struggle in school at first, but by the time he was thirteen, with my constant encouragement, Franco was really enjoying learning. We had a convention at church, and he participated in it. He stood tall and performed recitation his teacher had given him.

Franco came to me later, and I asked him if he knew Jesus, if he was saved. He said yes, he was saved, and that he loved Jesus. I could see that he meant it. In fact, the best revivals we have ever had at CHO have been when Franco preached them for us. He is a man in God's Word.

He completed his studies and graduated from the eighth grade at our school, which was the end of the schooling we could provide. But Franco wanted to go to a Christian high school, which was located downtown.

With my help, and the help of his mother, one of his former teachers, and other CHO friends, we managed to pay for his tuition, books and uniforms. Franco's desire was fulfilled, and he had the best education available anywhere in Haiti.

When he graduated from high school at age twenty-one, Franco came to me again and said, "Mom, I have finished high school, and I want to go to medical school. But I have no money to go." I could not help him anymore, and neither could his former teacher. "Jesus can help you go to medical school," I told Franco.

"I'm going to pray for God to make a way for me to go to medical school," he told me. I promised him I would agree in prayer with him for that.

When Franco took the admissions test for the

government-run medical school in downtown Port-au-Prince, he passed the test and was accepted. The Haitian government does not allow their medical students to study overseas, but they do bring in professors from all over the world to teach medicine in Haiti. And so Franco would be able to study medicine here.

Little by little, the money began to come in for Franco's medical school expenses. Funds came from us, from others I told about his need, and from friends in America. No one was able to provide large sums of money, but small amounts came in from many sources for Franco's needs to be met. We did a lot of fasting and praying, and Franco did whatever he could to have food and to make ends meet.

It seemed like every semester he would start, I would say to him, "Franco, this looks like the last semester you will be able to study, because we don't have the money to send you back anymore. The money just isn't here." And of course we were tired from having to try so hard to find the money for his studies.

But every semester, Franco would come to me and say, "Mom, be my prayer partner about this need, and let's see what God will do." So we would pray, and trust, and wait to see what He would do. Every time we prayed, God opened a new door, a new avenue for meeting Franco's needs. The money always came; sometimes it was the very last day it could possibly come in. Sometimes it even came in days after the deadline, and he would show up at the school to see if they would still let him register. They always did.

Franco was living at home with his mother while he studied medicine, and many times he would have to walk for as many as six hours, sometimes in the rain, to get to and from school every day.

When he told me about his plight, I decided to give him a place to stay in our compound at the orphanage. I have four two-room houses in the complex, which I have named Matthew, Mark, Luke and John. I let him live in Mark, unit A, for four years while attending medical school.

We let him study in the church so he could have light to read by, even though the one light bulb was too dim and too high up for him to see the pages easily. He often stayed through the night, and we would find him there, still studying, when we came in for early morning prayer at 5:30. Day after day Franco would study until the early hours of the morning, then sleep for three hours, and leave to make his way downtown for his day's classes.

Sunday, October 20, 1996, was the day Franco graduated from medical school. Though I could not be there, I sent one of our CHO workers from Margate to take videos and represent me and CHO. Franco had no money to pay for a class ring, or even for a cap and gown in which to participate in the ceremony. But I took money from my pension fund and paid for those things for him. What a day that was!

Shortly after Franco's graduation, I heard about a medical conference at Jackson Memorial Hospital in Florida that I wanted him to attend in order to improve his professional credentials and expertise. I called a woman doctor I knew in Miami, and she was able to get Franco registered to attend the conference. We were able to come up with the money to purchase the airline ticket for him to fly to Miami.

In the meantime, I went to a medical supply store and bought Franco a stethoscope, a blood pressure gauge and some other pieces of medical equipment he needed to practice. He had no bag for carrying these things, so he used a paper bag. In this bag he also carried his passport.

One day, not long before Franco was to leave for the conference, someone grabbed his paper bag as he rode the public transport in Port-au-Prince. The man ran off the bus before Franco could do anything about it. Franco called me, crying, and said, "Mom, all is lost; I can't go to the conference! Someone stole my bag, and my passport is gone, and now I can't go."

I said to him, "Franco, don't cry! God knows exactly where your passport is and who took it." I reminded him that, as the scripture says, "The king's heart is in the hand of the LORD; he directs it like a watercourse wherever he pleases" (Proverbs 21:1 NIV).

Franco was dejected, and I had a hard time convincing him that all was not lost. He kept saying that someone had stolen his passport and that he would never see it again. "I didn't hear one word you just said!" I told him, "but you must hear what I just said: The king's heart is in the Lord's hand, and God will direct as He pleases," I repeated.

"Okay, Mom, I am not crying anymore," he said, finally. "What do I do now? How can I get to the conference?"

"You can't get there without a passport; you have to have that. You will have to get your passport back. You will get it back," I told him.

"Oh, Mom, I don't know about that," he kept saying.

"Don't say that again, I don't want to hear that," I reminded him. "Go to the embassy tomorrow morning."

"But they don't have it — I lost it on the street, not at the embassy," he argued.

"Don't talk — stop talking," I told him firmly. "Just go to the embassy tomorrow. And whatever you do, don't talk negatively. Whatever you say, say only positive things."

I am not sure how much sleep he got that night, but he did go to the embassy the next day, and his faith must have been stronger by the time he got there. "My passport is here," he announced to the embassy worker after he entered the building. "I dropped my passport yesterday, and I lost it. It is here."

The embassy worker objected, insisting that they had no passports there. As the two were discussing back and forth, a man waiting there spoke up and said to the embassy worker, "Listen, he is just asking you to pull out your drawer and look for his passport; just look for it! That's all he is asking you to do."

And so, reluctantly, the worker began to look on his desk and through the drawers. In the second drawer he pulled out to look through, he found two passports. *One was Franco's!* Apparently, the person who had stolen Franco's bag had looked at the passport, saw that he was a doctor, became fearful, decided not to keep it and turned it in to the embassy.

God had worked dramatically and quickly, and Franco caught the plane to Miami. There he was met by officials from the conference who took him where he needed to go. Soon afterwards someone bought him a proper bag for his equipment, which we had to replace. He also was able to get a small backpack for carrying his things when he has to walk into the jungle to give medical treatment to families who live in villages far from the cities.

The doctors at the medical school where Franco studied met in December of 1996 to decide where Franco should do his required one-year internship after graduation. They were upset with him, jealous maybe, that he had gotten to go to the conference outside of Haiti, and they assigned him to practice medicine at a place called La Badee which is near Cap Haitien — not an easy assignment.

Cap Haitien is the place where Haitians built a Citadel on the northern coast after their independence in 1804, to guard against a possible French invasion. Franco went for a year to practice medicine in the villages in that area. Though Cap Haitien is a tourist attraction for foreigners, the local people are desperately poor and unable to afford medical care in their unsanitary living conditions. Many children live on the street and have no real place to call home — not even a place to sleep where they can be protected from the elements. They eat whatever food they find in the garbage, even if it is covered with flies and roaches.

Because there is no medical care in that area, this was a good experience for Franco. The poverty-stricken people there suffer from many different diseases, and Franco had to make all decisions by himself as to how to treat them. It was a trial by fire in many ways.

Franco came down from the Cap Haitien area

periodically to check with his advisors at the medical school and to get their input on problems he had seen, and so he learned from them while his work continued in the villages. His access to medicines was limited, so we helped him as much as we could with provision for the needs he saw. Franco took his mother to stay with him during his internship in Cap Haitien. This kept the local women from latching onto him in hopes that they could marry a doctor.

Today Franco is studying for his final medical exams in the U.S. When he passes the tests he will return to CHO as a doctor for our community in Port-au-Prince, and for our children in Jeremie. We truly planted seeds into good soil.

10
Outreach to Haitian Pastors

Through the Lord's mercies we are not consumed, because His compassions fail not. They are new every morning; great is Your faithfulness.

Lamentations 3:22-23 NKJV

Haitian pastors and church members come down from the mountains for the convention we hold every year in July. Many times we've had pastors who had to sleep on the ground in the garage area. I put cardboard down and spread sheets on the cardboard, and said to the men, "This is the best I can do. I'm sorry, but this is your accommodations."

Some of them began to weep. The man in charge said, "Mamma, they are not crying because it's miserable; they're crying because they're looking at nice, clean, lovely sheets. Some of these men are going to sleep on a sheet tonight for the first time in their entire lives."

A friend of mine who worked at a hotel had made it known to the housekeeping supervisor that she knew of a missionary in Haiti who was so short of sheets, that the children were put to bed on cardboard or on whatever they could find such as torn diapers. She asked this person for the sheets which were not top quality for guests sleeping in the hotel. To our amazement, the hotel gave us two hundred lovely white sheets. Some of them had nail polish or other little stains that kept them from being at their best for the hotel, but otherwise were in good condition. They gave them to us nicely ironed and packed in boxes.

We sent the sheets to Haiti just in time for me to put a sheet down on the cardboard for each pastor who was there for the convention. They were so thrilled that I gave each man his sheet to take home with him. We again had a shortage of sheets, but praise the Lord, we were short for a good reason!

Not long after that, I began praying about beds. I wanted to do something better than the cardboard on the ground, and I said that to Jesus in my prayer time. I asked Him to bless us with a way to put all those men down to sleep without having to have them on the ground again.

The wonderful thing about Jesus is that He answers prayer. We don't pray and walk away hoping He or somebody heard it somewhere. But we pray knowing that God hears and answers prayer. About four or five hours after my prayer time the phone rang. A man said to me "We're not far from you — the Days Inn Motel. I don't know what you do, but we found you listed in the yellow pages, and I wondered if you could use some beds."

Well, I was shocked, speechless. I said, "You did say 'beds,' didn't you?"

He said, "Yes, I said, 'beds.'"

I said, "Sir, I'm in my house praying that God will provide some way for me to have beds in Haiti for pastors who come to our place to listen to American pastors and evangelists and missionaries in seminars and workshops."

He replied, "Lady, if you want the beds, I am right here," and he told me how to find his location. "Please come down and we can talk."

I called my driver, we jumped in the van and drove to where the man was. He had more than we could carry away on our little van, so we rented a truck and went back to that Days Inn Motel. They gave us sixty-nine beds and sixty-nine mattresses.

We came away just rejoicing and praising the Lord. It took a lot of doing to get them to Miami and arrange to fly them down to Haiti. But we were energized because God had so marvelously answered prayer. We paid the shipping fees to get them on the flight, and then paid whatever was necessary on the other end to get them out of customs in Haiti.

One hundred twenty men came to the convention that year. We just left the beds in the garage area, separated the box spring from the mattress and instead of accommodating 69 people, we accommodated 138 people. We used cinder blocks with plywood on top to raise up the mattress to the height of a bed. This made a very comfortable bed. And for the box spring we did the same thing. We got sheets and blankets and made up those beds and made those people comfortable.

We went from cardboard on the concrete ground to 138 beds. We accommodated every one of the pastors and their wives, though in some cases we had the women in one section and the men in another. The small children slept with their mothers. The older children slept on pallets on the floor of the orphanage. It was wonderful and marvelous to see God's provision and how "right on" He is. He just does not fail! He'll meet us wherever we are.

At convention time every year I noticed that many pastors did not have shoes, or they were wearing tennis shoes with holes in them. Many had the soles gone, and were flapping or were being held together with a rubber band around the ball of the foot. And they come walking, many of them. They would walk during the day and sleep under a tree at night, or with friends all along the way. They would make that four-day walk.

Some of them had money enough to ride the tap-tap — a public mode of transportation that goes into the villages in the mountains. It's the main means of transportation in Haiti. Like a Greyhound bus would be here. But as you can imagine, these truck-type vehicles are far less comfortable than a Greyhound bus. But the Pastors come because they're so hungry for the Word. They're hungry to know what Jesus is saying to them, how to prepare themselves for the Lord's return and how to bring people to salvation.

We bring in American pastors and Bible teachers, Sunday school teachers, missionaries and church workers. During the seminars and workshops for the four days of the convention, these Haitian workers learn a lot.

One morning in early June I was praying in my special place of prayer, and l lifted the pastors' needs before the Lord. "God, I need about 500 pairs of shoes to bless these men and their wives, and their children. I don't know where I would get that many shoes, but You do. Lord, You know I couldn't buy the shoes even if they were only five dollars a pair. That would be a wonderful bargain if they were new shoes. I would want to do it, but I would be limited. So Lord, I'm just going to thank You for providing me with 500 pairs of shoes for men and women and children, and babies."

To my utter amazement — while I was praying and praising the Lord, the telephone rang right at my elbow. I reached over and picked it up and said, "Hello."

A man said to me, "I'm Dr. Michael. I wonder if you could use a lot of shoes." Now, that was so shocking that I just sat there for a moment trying to make sure of what I had heard. He said, "Hello? Are you there?"

"Yes, sir," I replied. "I'm blown away by what you just asked me."

"Well, why?" he asked.

"Because right now, I'm still sitting in my place of prayer," I told him. "I've been praying that God would somehow provide for me to have shoes for pastors in Haiti who will be coming out of the mountains for our convention next month, July."

He said, "Well, I just need to know if you would like to have them."

"Oh, yes, I'd love to have them," I answered quickly. Then he gave me his address and the location.

I hung the phone up and ran through the house for Anna, our secretary, who lived here in the house with me at that time. I woke her abruptly and said, "Get dressed! There's no time for a shower or anything else, just come on. You gotta go with me."

"Well, where are we going in such a hurry?" she asked. I told her what the doctor had said, and gave her the address we were headed for.

In about ten minutes we were in the van and in the

station wagon. Now the van is seldom ever there that early in the morning. Usually our driver, Brother James, takes it with him to Miami. But this day the van was parked in front of the house, so I drove the station wagon and Anna took the van. We took off to find this doctor at a hospital in the city of Plantation, Florida.

Before he had hung up, I had asked, "Doctor, please tell me, how did you get my name? And how do I know you?"

"You don't know me," he answered. "I picked up your name in the yellow pages. I'm a podiatrist, and we just had a fund-raiser banquet to add a wing to the hospital. The other doctors had to share in this, and I asked people invited to the banquet to bring a pair of shoes with them to give away. We've been inundated with shoes at the hospital, and they're in the way. We just need them to be moved. We ask that you not sell the shoes, but make them available free of cost to the poor in Haiti."

"Well, you made the right phone call, at the right time, to the right person," I told him. "God is answering my prayer!"

"Well, lady, if you want these shoes, you'd better get over here," he had said somewhat impatiently.

We found the place. There he was standing in the doorway waiting when we arrived. Inside we saw bin after bin after bin, piled to the very top with shoes. All sizes, all shapes. Shoes for men, shoes for women and shoes for children. It was amazing.

We filled the station wagon and we filled the van with shoes, until we barely could see to drive. We had to peek over the shoes to see how to back out, and peek out of the side windows to drive back to the house. We came back rejoicing.

I tried to say something to that doctor concerning Jesus, but he was too busy. He didn't want any part of that, he just wanted me to take the shoes and go. So we prayed for him as we left. I wrote him a nice thank you letter. When we arrived home with the shoes I dropped to my knees and Anna and I began to count them, pair by pair.

That man gave us 1,000 pair of shoes. He doubled what I had asked from the Lord. Well, we had quite a time packing shoes into boxes. But we made them secure and labeled them and sent them to Haiti by Haiti Air Freight.

It was an awful lot of hard work to get all that done. But we did it, because we know the gift is nothing unless we're willing to follow through so the gift can do exactly what it was meant to do. The shoes were there in time for the convention to help those men who came out of the mountains, wanting to hear the Word, wanting to understand the Word, wanting to know how to rightly divide the Word. They went back to the mountains after the convention, rejoicing and praising the Lord, each with a pair of shoes that fit them.

As we were packing things in, we found nine different odd shoes without mates. The doctor had said, "These are all odd shoes. Would you have need for these?"

I said, "Oh, yes, sir. I'll take all nine." He gave them to me.

When I got to Haiti I was able to satisfy all those men and women who came to the convention and send some of the men home with shoes for their wives, if they knew their sizes for shoes. There was one special man, pastoring a church in the mountains. When he was eleven years old, a tree fell on him and he lost his leg. They had cut it off with an axe, then he'd had surgery and it healed up. But for thirty-eight years — now he was forty-nine years old — he had had only one leg. He made his own crutches. But he never missed the convention, even though he had to walk that distance. He knew how to use his crutches and drop down from one rock to another, and land safely onto a rock. He knew how to choose exactly the right one.

There among a thousand pairs of shoes was one shoe for the right foot, and it was just the perfect size for this pastor. We were rejoicing, because even the man with one foot was satisfied with a shoe.

When Jesus does it, it's flawless, it's perfect. And all we can say is, "Praise God, from Whom all blessings flow!"

11
God Is Never Late

> **Behold, I am the Lord, the God of all flesh. Is there anything too hard for Me?...Call to Me, and I will answer you, and show you great and mighty things, which you do not know.**
>
> **Jeremiah 32:27; 33:3 NKJV**

In 1991 the Social Welfare Department of Haiti brought nine babies to us who were HIV positive. They were so desperately ill that I had to separate them from the rest of the children. Our Haitian workers don't always give a lot of attention to hygienic matters in the nursery, so I had to make sure that these babies were by themselves. A careless error could cause other babies to be infected, so we took extra precautions.

We put the HIV babies in a house down the street from the orphanage and hired people to work only in that location. Also, we gave them special training to take care of these precious little ones. They did all the laundry for these babies instead of sending their things to the orphanage laundry, and they cleaned and scrubbed the house daily inside and out. The area outside the house is all cement — no dirt anywhere except out on the street — so it was easier to keep free of dust.

Though some of these babies did not respond to anything we did for them, we kept praying and believing in the healing power of the Lord. Certainly they were not the first "hopeless cases" we had taken in. After a period of time some of the babies began responding to our care, but several months from the time they came to us, two of them went to be with Jesus.

We continued praying every day and presenting the remaining seven babies to Him, believing for them to be healed in the name of Jesus. We took them to a clinic in Port-au-Prince to be tested to determine the status of their condition. The doctors there said, "Yes, these babies are HIV positive." So we took them back and continued to present them to the Lord to let Him know that our faith was still in Him.

After a few months we took the babies to be tested again by the same doctors at the same clinic. No change. We went a third time and got the same report. They were still HIV positive. But we never stopped praying and thanking God for His healing power. The babies were eating fairly well, and growing, so I believed we were making progress with them.

Again we took them to be tested, but this time to a different place than before. "There is something strange happening here," the doctor said. "I don't know exactly what to call it." Finally he said he would call it a "low positive." Even though we didn't understand it, we just knew God was working in these babies. Praise His holy name!

We stepped up our prayer and praise for these precious little ones and God continued His faithfulness to us. Time kept marching on. A few months later we took the babies to a third clinic near Port-au-Prince for an HIV test. The doctor took the blood test of one of the babies. In a little while he came back into the room and said, "This baby has tested negative." How we rejoiced at that report!

Precious little LeeAnn, the oldest of the HIV babies, was completely healed and went from positive to negative. Two men who had come from a church in Oregon to visit the orphanage stayed across from the HIV house. The windows of these two houses face each other with a small walkway in between. One of these men told me that in the middle of the night he would wake up and would hear LeeAnn singing praises to Jesus in French — and this was before she was healed of the HIV virus.

Now, several years later, she attends school with all the other children. She is a very bright, happy child, and has an eagerness to learn about the ways of Jesus. LeeAnn is a real testimony to what God is doing in the land of Haiti. I know God has a special ministry waiting for her.

Eventually all the remaining HIV positive babies tested negative, and one of them was adopted by an American family. At this writing we no longer have any HIV babies at the orphanage, but the Social Welfare workers know we will take them anytime they have such children who need to be cared for. It is hard to put into words the praises that flow from my spirit when our faithfulness to the Lord is blessed by such answers to prayer.

Desks for Our School

The needs of our school and orphanage were increasing at such a rate it was difficult to stay ahead. Our school children were having to stand or sit on the floor during school sessions because we had no benches or chairs for them. We needed wood for my carpenters to build these things, but we had no funds for buying lumber.

While I was in Columbus, Ohio, at one of my speaking engagements, I shared with the people that my children didn't have any chairs to sit on while they attended class. At that conference was a woman who worked as secretary to the head of the State Department of Education. She went to her boss and told him what she heard me share about the need in Haiti, and reminded him of the warehouse full of used desks. These things had come from a school that was being remodeled, and the old furnishings were being replaced with brand new things. She asked her boss if the missionary from Haiti could have these desks and chairs for her school.

He said yes, on the condition we would pick them up and arrange to transport them. I called James at our Margate office, and he drove to Columbus to see what needed to be done. When he saw how many desks and chairs were involved, he decided it would take three eighteen-wheel moving vans to take the desks and chairs to Margate for preparation for shipment to Haiti. That would cost $1,800, which we didn't have, so I began to pray. The Lord impressed me to call the pastors who had attended the conference where I had just spoken and tell them of my need. They shared it with their congregations and responded immediately. We were able to hire two vans to bring our desks and chairs to Margate. By carefully stacking the pieces into the moving vans, they got everything loaded into two vans instead of three, which saved us $600.

We inventoried the desks and chairs, had them

loaded into a container in Miami, and shipped them to Haiti for use in our school. We moved the containers to the school compound to distribute the furniture among the classrooms and the offices of the school and the orphanage. We even had enough desks to give to some of the small schools in our community. When the Lord blesses us we also bless those around us who have needs.

God's Provision

One summer not long before time for our July convention, I found out about an international feeding service called Food for the Poor, and called them to ask for help for our work in Haiti. They supply rice and beans and other staples to organizations working in third-world countries. The man I spoke with told me they had no more supplies on hand for charitable organizations like CHO. But then he explained how he could arrange for me to purchase rice for only $8.00 per hundred pounds — while at that time in Haiti one hundred pounds of rice cost $62. Only one problem: I would have to buy several tons of rice and pay for it in advance, a total $3,200. I had no money, but told the man, "Yes, I'll take it."

"What?" exclaimed Anna, one of our CHO office workers who was sitting beside me. "Where are we going to get that much money?"

"I don't know," I told her. "But Jesus knows our every need — the problem belongs to Him." We went back to Margate and praised God for the $3,200 that He was going to give us over and above our already strained budget. Two days later the phone rang just after our prayer time, as it often does — God answering our need through the telephone. A pastor from a church in California was on the phone and said, "Mom, we're coming to the convention, and as always we're bringing $2,000 to help with food." Then he asked whether he should send it ahead, or bring it with him.

"Oh, please send it, send it," I answered. "If it has to do with food send it right away." I explained to him the opportunity we had, and that we needed the money immediately. "It's on the way," he promised. Over the next couple of days the rest of the needed money came in. We were able to pay for the rice and pay for shipping it to Haiti in time for the convention. We fed everyone for those four days, and sent all the pastors and workers home with a supply of rice.

A short time later an embargo against Haiti caused an already starving nation to struggle even more. Often when these things happen the government closes all the schools, which means that children who usually attend our school and have a meal provided for them, have nothing to eat. We were able to give out rice in twenty-pound cans to families who live around our compound. These people already are dirt poor and can barely afford to provide for their children even when food is available. What a blessing to be able to help them during such difficult times.

Eyeglasses Provided

Another time an eye technician from the University of California at Los Angeles heard me speak at a fund-raiser for the orphanage. After the meeting she talked to me at length about coming to Haiti to conduct an eye clinic. She gathered 900 pairs of eyeglasses, then four other doctors to help. They came to Haiti and set up a clinic at the church on our compound and were able to examine five people at a time. By the end of the day all the glasses had been given out. The doctors were so excited about the project, they promised to return and bring 2,000 pairs of glasses.

We try to see to it that the Haitians who attend our church have a Bible of their own. Sometimes I see a woman with a Bible on her lap, but it may be upside down, or turned to the wrong book, or opened to just any page to make it look good. Most of the time it is because they don't see well, and need glasses. It is really sad to see this over and over again throughout the congregation. If only they had glasses they could follow the teaching so much better and grow in the Lord. These people are just happy to have a Bible whether they can read it well or not.

Here Comes the Bride

As we study God's Word and share it with the people in Haiti we discover their real needs. We help them to understand God's Word so they can apply this knowledge to their everyday lives and their needs are met. Through the seminars and workshops many of the Haitian pastors and church leaders come to realize they are living in sin, because they are raising families without being married.

Whenever I discover such a circumstance I go to the individuals and tell them this practice isn't biblical, then explain to them what the Bible says about marriage. Sometimes the woman will cry. The man usually dwells on the negatives, reminding me of the high cost of having a wedding. "We can't pay for the ring, the marriage license, proper clothes to wear...."

"Listen," I say, "let me talk for a moment. Jesus has sent me to help the people of Haiti — people just like you. Jesus loves you and I love you, and together we are going to teach you the righteous ways of God and help you obey Him by taking the vows of holy matrimony."

The first step is to provide money for them to go back to their villages and acquire a birth certificate or baptismal certificate. They must have something showing they are Haitian that identifies their birthplace and date of birth. Then I have to buy their marriage license. Finally, after working on all these things needed to get married, we plan the wedding and find a pastor to marry them in the church on our compound. Sometimes we allow them to take baths in our facilities, because of lack of water and soap at home. Most of the time we have someone help the ladies do their hair and apply a little makeup.

Because I have shared about this problem while speaking in the states, many CHO friends have given me veils, wedding dresses, or nice dresses that are suitable for a wedding. I've also asked people to help by supplying rings for these weddings. We have in storage several different styles and sizes of wedding dresses. The brides especially like the gowns with veils and long trains. We want our brides and grooms to feel that when they obey God's Word, they can have a wedding that's really special for them.

The bonding of two people together also calls for exchanging rings, but our Haitian brides and grooms cannot afford rings for their ceremony. At one wedding I witnessed the groom giving his bride a cigar band for a wedding ring. I thought about people in the states who have rings they never wear, while these people in Haiti are using anything that resembles a ring to complete their marriage vows. So I began asking for rings.

Whenever a wedding is about to be performed we bring the bride and groom up to my room to measure their fingers and fit them for a ring. I can't tell you the delight in the eyes of these brides and grooms when we give them rings. It is like that final tie that binds them together.

One day we had nine brides, and because of the help of so many CHO friends, we had a dress for each one. Some of these brides had five or six children who marched in with them, but I was delighted that they were taking this step of obedience to God's Word. (Of course every bride would love to keep the dress she wears for her wedding, but we insist that she leave the bridal clothes with us so we're prepared the next time we need to plan a wedding.)

On this particular day, everyone looked wonderful in their wedding apparel — except that two men were barefoot. They had worn their old tennis shoes down from the mountains for the ceremony, but didn't have shoes to wear for the occasion, so they were in their bare feet. I spoke to one man who was standing outside the church waiting for his cue. "Brother, where are your shoes?" I asked.

Almost in tears he said, "Mom, I don't have shoes to wear down the aisle. All I have is those old tennis shoes, and they just don't look good with my new suit and shirt."

I looked around — I am always looking around, it seems — and saw an American pastor standing nearby. He was in the right place at the right time! I ran over to him and said, "Pastor, let me see your shoes." He was so surprised he didn't quite know how to respond. Finally he asked, "Why do you want to see my shoes?"

"Quick, quick — let me see your shoes. What size are they?" Then I told him of the plight of the groom and how he needed a pair of shoes immediately. The pastor agreed to lend his shoes, and when the groom slipped his feet into them, they were just the right size. Another visiting American pastor also volunteered his shoes for the second barefoot man. As the wedding party walked into the church everyone was dressed so nicely. That is, except for two American pastors who were now in stocking feet!

Over the years the love and the grace of our Lord have never failed. We have trusted in Him with all our needs, and have found Him to be true to His Word. Day by day and even hour by hour God has been faithful to me and to the ministry of CHO. Because His love is so great it reaches even to the people of Haiti — a country that a misguided leader long ago dedicated to the devil. We know God's will is for them to find deliverance and then walk in His truth.

12

Facing a New Challenge

If you extend your soul to the hungry
And satisfy the afflicted soul,
Then your light shall dawn in the darkness,
And your darkness shall be as the noonday.

Isaiah 58:10 NKJV

In 1992 the people of Haiti experienced a great tragedy off the coast of Jeremie, a small town on the southwest side of the island about 200 miles from Port-au-Prince. It is possible to travel this distance by car, but the condition of the road is simply indescribable. Under "normal" conditions, the trip will take about nine hours. At certain places the roads are washed out and you can't get through except with a four-wheel-drive vehicle. There are great potholes that will flatten the newest of tires in an instant. Nylon tires are the only tires that can hold up on a trip such as this.

The road has no guardrails. When you drive around a blind curve with a steep ravine on the side of the road, you have to use extreme caution for another vehicle may be approaching without warning. The road was built by peasants with picks and shovels and is maintained the same way. Certain mountain passes are so narrow that only one vehicle can pass at a time. At times one vehicle will have to back up quite some distance in order to let the other one pass.

Some truck drivers have to stop their trucks and check the side of the road to be sure the shoulder is strong enough to support the weight of the load. If the truck is too long to maneuver a narrow curve, the driver may spend a couple of hours reinforcing the edge of the road with large rocks so the wheels may pass without incident.

A much faster way to travel between Port-au-Prince and Jeremie is by ferry boat. The trip normally takes two to three hours if the sea is smooth and the load on the ferry is secure. Farmers and merchants would transport their goods for sale or trade from the mountains around Jeremie to the market in Port-au-Prince. Wood carvings, tin pots, charcoal for cooking, goats, pigs, chickens and anything else that might bring revenue.

Imagine a New York ferry loaded beyond its capacity, three levels high, during the rush hour of the day. The load includes cars, trucks, people and animals. Also vendors selling food and drink and every trinket imaginable. All levels are filled beyond capacity. No one gives attention to safety precautions. This describes the typical Haitian ferry.

Tragedy struck the Jeremie ferry without warning one day when a storm with very high waves arose and began rocking the boat. The people on board began to panic and were moving from side to side. No one heard the captain of the vessel announce a warning to stay in one place and remain calm. The ferry overturned and thousands of people drowned. It was the worst tragedy in Haiti's history, and it left thousands of children orphaned in the coastal town of Jeremie.

At the time of this accident I was on a speaking tour in the U.S. to raise money for our orphanage in

Mariani. One day as I ended my prayer time God spoke to my heart very clearly that I was to go to Jeremie and start an orphanage to help take care of the hundreds of children who were orphaned by this terrible ferry accident. Immediately I began making preliminary arrangements by phone. I instructed the men working for CHO to get our bus ready for that treacherous road trip — especially by getting sturdy new tires.

My speaking engagements over, I returned to Haiti to prepare the team of workers who would join me for the trip. The cooks prepared food and we filled several five gallon jugs with water to drink along the way. Our baker baked fresh bread and we stored it in boxes and put them in the bus. We took blankets and pillows for the overnight stay on the road. We committed the whole trip to the Lord and asked Him to cover us with His blood as we went.

Along this road there are no gas stations, so when you come to a place with barrels that look like they may contain gasoline, you stop. We stopped at a particular place and asked the attendant to fill our tank with gas. When he took a quart-sized saucepan, dipped it into his gas barrel and began pouring it through a funnel into our tank, we knew we were in for a long wait. We made good use of our time by sharing Jesus with the people from the mountains as they walked by the bus.

Most of the Haitians who came by had never heard the name of Jesus before this day. Many of the women who stopped to listen were carrying great loads on their heads, on their way back from the market to their homes up in the mountains. Nevertheless they would take time to stop and listen to us sing or talk about Jesus. Very seldom did we see a man carrying anything on his head.

The men usually work with their hands — digging with shovels or hoes, or cutting brush with a machete. Some of them work with knives carving objects from wood to sell in the marketplace.

All along this narrow mountain road we saw men, women and small children sharing the narrow road with the cars and large trucks. At times pedestrians would stop close to the edge of the canyon side of the road to allow vehicles to pass, hoping the driver could see them so they wouldn't be hurled down the ravine. Along the way were many vendors selling goods of every description — pots and pans, wood carvings, charcoal, fruits, vegetables and many other items related to the mountain people. Since no rest stops existed along this road, we had to do what the mountain people do when needed.

On one trip to Jeremie we saw a large truck that hadn't made it around a sharp curve, and it had tumbled into one of the small canyons. The men living in a small mountain village nearby took the truck apart and hoisted the pieces with very crude hoists back up to the road. Such accidents can happen several times along the way. These are some of the reasons that the trip from Port-au-Prince to Jeremie by car takes so long.

After a grueling ten hours of bouncing up and down, side to side and forward and back, we arrived at our destination: Jeremie. It was seven o'clock in the evening and the sun was setting as we pulled up to the police station and went into the humble little building to get our papers checked. On the porch was a rickety old chair bearing the telltale signs of a police force without a budget. Over in one corner a soldier sat at an old desk. We explained to him the purpose of our visit while his assistant checked our bus with my Haitian driver. Everything seemed to meet with the soldier's approval, so we were free to enter the town of Jeremie.

The first night we had planned to sleep in the bus by spreading out blankets on the floor between the seats. But after considering the cramped conditions I decided to inquire about town for a motel. It didn't take long to find the only motel in Jeremie. It was built into the side of a mountain with stairs to the entrance so steep we had to hang on to the railing for fear of falling backward. But at the top was the most beautiful view of the Caribbean Sea I had ever seen. We hired a man to bring water to our rooms for our needs, then we ate some of the food we'd brought with us and retired for the night.

The next morning we went around the small town of Jeremie talking to different people regarding the conditions of the children who had been orphaned by that terrible ferry accident. There were children sleeping in the street under any kind of shelter they could find. Children were crying all night for the parents who will never come home. As we heard more and more stories about these children trying to fend for themselves, God confirmed to my heart what my next step was to be. We went to the Social Welfare Department, and I explained who I was and gave a brief resume of my work in Port-au-Prince. The workers could not believe we would take our time to drive all the way to their small town to inquire about the suffering children who had been orphaned. It didn't take long to convince them that we came because Jesus wanted us to take these children in our arms and give them love, and provide for their needs.

They told us about one family of nine children

desperately needing a place to stay. The director continued to tell us about case after case of children who were living on the street. Listening to her gave us a better understanding of what God wanted us to do. By faith, I told the director it would be possible in the future for us to take about fifty children, but first we needed to find a house to rent. She promptly closed her office and went with us to look for a place.

Hours later, most of the day had been spent and still we had no place to rent. Since we were supposed to leave early the next morning for Port-au-Prince, my driver kept urging me to return to our motel. But I declared, "No, we will find a place to rent." As the evening sun began to set I prayed, "God, I know You have a perfect place for us — please guide me." Then I was quiet before the Lord.

At a busy intersection we were waiting in our bus for the traffic to move. A car coming from the opposite direction had to stop just opposite my window, which was open. The gentleman in the car looked up and said, "I'm going to take a chance and ask you something — are you Mom Workman?"

"Yes," I answered, "but how do you know me?" He explained that he had heard of my work in Haiti but had never met me personally. He said he and his family had been in Jeremie as missionaries for the past six years. When he mentioned he was willing to help me, I told him where we were staying, and suggested he could pick me up there later.

In the middle of dinner I heard him drive up to the door, so I jumped up, put on my coat and ran out to the car. We left the dusty streets of Jeremie and headed up into the mountains. I thought the roads we already had driven on were bad, but never in my life had I seen a road in this condition. I prayed every inch of the way.

As we approached the property the missionary stopped the car, jumped out and opened an old gate. As we drove toward an old weathered house my heart saw what God wanted for me in Jeremie. Standing before me in the semi-darkness was everything I needed to make the children of Jeremie happy. There were fruit trees, a place for a garden and a place for the children to play. "God," I prayed, "You have placed everything right here — this is what I need. Thank You!"

When we walked toward the front of the house, the missionary made a certain sound and a man came running to the front of the house to open the door. When we went inside they used matches to light the rooms as we moved about looking through the house. I asked for the owner and was told he was running a mechanics shop in Port-au-Prince. We thanked the man and returned to the motel, as it was very late in the evening. My plate was on the table, covered and awaiting my return. I got all the information about the house and its owner from Paul, the missionary, and throughout the night I was praising my God for guiding me just as I had asked Him to do.

All the properties I had looked at during my stay in Jeremie were $1,500 a month to rent, which was more than we could afford. As soon as they heard my English the prices of the properties soared beyond belief. "I'm not trying to live in luxury — I'm trying to take your children off the streets and feed them," I told some of them. But most of the landlords didn't care about the children; they only cared about money. After comparing all the other places with the place Paul had showed me, I knew which one I wanted for the children from the streets of Jeremie.

"The place has been abandoned for five years, but it rents for three hundred a month," Paul had told me. "If the landlord wants more, you tell him 'No, Paul says it rents for three hundred a month.'"

When I arrived back in Port-au-Prince I couldn't wait to speak with the owner of that property. I located him in the downtown area, and learned he was a part owner of the ferry that capsized. We talked for a few minutes, then I mentioned that I wanted to rent his property in Jeremie. "Paul told me it rents for three hundred a month," I said.

"I could choke that Paul," the man replied, and we laughed about it for awhile. But I was delighted that he allowed me to rent it for a whole year at that rate by paying in advance.

On our second trip to Jeremie we took beds, sheets, pillows, and a lot of other things to make our stay more comfortable. We had the neighbors come in and clean the place to make it more presentable, and I used my own workers to begin the remodeling. The place needed wiring, plumbing, and other major work just to make the house livable. But I knew it would be a beautiful place for the children.

Before leaving on my return trip to Port-au-Prince I went back to talk to the Social Welfare director about the fifty children we planned to take. I had to convince her that we could take only fifty at the start, but later would take more.

About this time the embargo hit and gas prices went up to $25.00 a gallon, so we couldn't return to Jeremie for awhile and the work stopped temporarily. But I chose two Haitian workers to be administrators and houseparents to the orphans. From Mariani we made all the preparations we possibly could, waiting for the day when we could return. Finally conditions improved and we went back and got the work underway.

By the time of this writing, we have purchased the Jeremie property. Fifty children are living there, with another fifteen coming to join the school-age orphanage children for school sessions and to receive meals. Our greatest problem has been to drill a deep, free-flowing well to provide a safe water supply to the orphanage. We are trusting God to help us finish it soon so the children no longer will have to hand-carry water to the house. When the water problem is solved, we hope to be able to take in more of the children the Social Welfare director has been urging us to take.

I came to Haiti more than twenty-five years ago to reach the little ones in its dusty streets — a place where one in five children has no chance of living past five years of age. These are children living in the dumps or under a tree who were abandoned by their parents — children whose mothers may have died and left them wandering in the streets trying to find food. These are the ones I came to reach to show them there is a life through Jesus Christ that can change all circumstances, even when we think life is hopeless. I wanted to point the children of Haiti to One Who loves them, One Who cares and understands every situation.

When we first began our school under a tree and asked the children "Who is Jesus?" not one of them knew. Today if you ask any of the five hundred-plus children in our Mariani school and orphanage you will get one answer: "Jesus is the Son of God." The children in Jeremie will give the same response. And if you go into the nursery and say "Jesus" to any of our toddlers, they will point their fingers toward heaven and repeat as best as they can, "Jesus."

Part of the vision God has given me for Haiti is in Jeremie, and it remains our greatest challenge. But He has energized my very being with His power to see it completed. I was seventy-five years young when the Jeremie project began, and at this writing I am seventy-nine years young. But God has a lot for me to do in this beautiful land. I think of Caleb at eighty asking God for the mountain, and God heard his prayer and gave him that mountain. I intend to be faithful to my Lord until He says, "Well done."

Appendix

Operating a ministry like Christian Haitian Outreach requires earnest prayer, shrewd planning, hard work, and trust in God. It also requires the help of many caring individuals, because I cannot do all the work myself. We do have staff who work regularly at the orphanage, but we also derive a great deal of benefit from groups and individuals who volunteer a week, a month, or as long as they can, to help us in whatever way they can.

Please consider volunteering to help us on a short-term or long-term basis at the orphanage in Haiti or in the Margate office. We can use you if you have office skills, if you can work with children, if you can help with maintenance or repair on our property, if you have medical training, or if you just want to help and are willing to be flexible and do whatever needs to be done.

With such a big "family" at CHO, it seems that I am always trying to cover expenses much greater than the CHO checking account contains. But God has always met our needs, many times through the generosity of those who care about us and can send money to pay for our regular, ongoing expenses or for special needs.

Will you help us with the expenses we incur in running our two orphanages? Please send your checks or money order to Christian Haitian Outreach, at the U.S. address given at the back of the book. You can earmark your gift for cribs and mattresses, for school supplies, for medicine for Dr. Franco's medical practice in Haiti, for legal costs for adoptions, or for whatever project interests you. Be assured that the money you send — all of it — will go to whatever project you designate. I give you my word on that.

In Haiti we have a constant need for food. Would you send funds to purchase it here, thus saving shipping costs? We can use multivitamins, formula, disposable diapers, over-the-counter medicines and baby products. We also need personal hygiene items such as hair products (shampoo, conditioner, and hair products suitable for black children), toothbrushes and toothpaste, soap, and other items. Try to think of items you use regularly or which you buy for your children's care, and those will likely be the same kinds of items we need for the children here as well.

For the school we are always in need of supplies for students such as paper, pencils and pens, rulers, notebooks, and the like. We also love to receive gifts of clothing, especially children's clothing, not only shirts and shoes but also the basics, like underwear and socks, washcloths and diapers.

The Bible says, "The prayer of a righteous man is powerful and effective" (James 5:16b NIV). Much of what we have seen God do with our work here at CHO has been the result of the constant prayer and praise which goes up toward heaven from our humble compound.

Will you pray for us? We like to let people know about the needs here, realizing that good people will want to know how to pray and how to help with the needs as well. Please pray for our protection at CHO, and for continual political stability for Haiti.

Please help us in whatever way you can. What you give to one of these children will come back to you many times better. As the scripture says, "Give, and it will be given to you. A good measure, pressed down, shaken together and running over, will be poured into your lap. For with the measure you use, it will be measured to you" (Luke 6:38 NIV).

Whether you help us by volunteering at the orphanage, by sending financial donations, by donating food or supplies, or by praying earnestly and regularly for the work here, it will be greatly appreciated.

— Eleanor Workman
Founder and President
Christian Haitian Outreach

Volunteer and Temporary Missionary Information

The principal objectives of Christian Haitian Outreach (CHO) are:

1. To provide support, housing, education and health care for the children living in the CHO orphanages in Mariani and in Jeremie.
2. To provide elementary education and one daily meal for approximately 600 children in the community around the CHO compound.
3. To train the people of Haiti to be strong men and women of God so that those held captive by Satan can be set free in Christ Jesus. Because of the voodoo background of this nation, it can be a long process to teach, train and bring the Haitian people from the dominion of darkness into the light of Jesus Christ.

Long-term workers at CHO must understand that as we work with the people of Haiti, it is not our purpose or intent to Americanize them. We strive to teach them the principles of God's Word within their own culture, including practical teaching in cleanliness, personal hygiene and grooming. Due to critical shortages of a clean water supply in Haiti, the danger of germs and disease is high, and cleanliness is difficult for the Haitians to achieve. Also, it is difficult for many of them even to understand why cleanliness is so important.

It is often equally difficult to teach the Haitian people the importance of completely breaking away from the influence of their voodoo background and from contact with their voodoo priest. Due to their lack of spiritual understanding and their fear of the voodoo priest, some Haitians remain too friendly with their previous friends and often fall back into their old habits and lifestyle.

For these reasons it is necessary that Eleanor Workman (the founder of the work, known to everyone as "Mom") keep a tight rein on the ministry at CHO. Mom Workman is the authority figure at CHO. In her absence, she will designate a staff person to act on her behalf. It is imperative that all CHO workers in Haiti prepare their hearts to accept this line of authority as unto the Lord, and to submit at all times to the instructions of Mom Workman. (Haitian workers are also expected to submit to this line of authority.)

It is possible that simple, well-meaning actions on the part of missionary staff members can violate accepted cultural behavior in Haiti and become an offense to those to whom we are attempting to minister. An incorrect action, a hasty word, or failure on the part of a sincere worker to follow instructions, has been known to damage the integrity and credibility of this ministry which can take months or years to restore. In learning to work with the Haitian CHO staff members, recognize that it takes time to earn their confidence and friendship. Also, remember that you need to be a good Christian example to them, as many of them are new Christians with very limited understanding of God's Word and Christian principles that we sometimes take for granted.

Missionary Application

Christian Haitian outreach, Inc.
P. O. Box 634545
Margate, FL 33063-4545

(To be filled out by all volunteers desiring to serve in Haiti)

Name_______________________ Occupation_________________

Address____________________ Phone #'s___________________

City/State/Zip ____

Personal Data:

Sex	Marital Status		Nationality
___Male	___ Married	___ Single	___ American
___Female	___ Divorced	___ Remarried	___ __________
	___ Widowed	___ Engaged	(other)

Birth Date____________ Place________________________ Age____

__Yes __No Do you have any chronic health problems or disabilities? If yes, please explain:

____

Christian Background

__Yes __No Have you accepted Jesus Christ as your personal Lord and Savior?
If yes, how long ago?__________________________

__Yes __No Have you received the baptism of the Holy Spirit according to Acts 2:4?
If yes, how long ago? __________________________

Name of church you attend_______________________________

Church address___________________________Phone___________

City/State/Zip ____

Pastor's Name____

___Yes ___No Are you a member?
How long have you been a member? _________
How long have you attended regularly?_________
In which areas of ministry have you participated?
____

___Yes ___No Have you held any leadership positions in the church? If so, describe briefly:_______________

__Yes ___No Have you ever used illegal drugs?
If yes, for how long?_______________________
Are you free of drugs now? ___Yes ___No

___Yes ___No Do you smoke?

___Yes ___No Do you drink alcoholic beverages?

___Yes ___No Have you ever been arrested?

If yes, please explain:_______________________

____

____

Personal References

Please provide the names of two people we can contact who know you well enough to give a character reference. Do not list relatives.

Name________________________________ Relationship________
Address ______________________________ Phone_____________
City/State/Zip____

Name________________________________ Relationship________
Address______________________________ Phone_____________
City/State/Zip____

Family Background

Father______________________ Mother______________________
Address______________________ Address______________________
City/State/Zip______________ City/State/Zip______________
Occupation_________________ Occupation_________________
Name of Spouse______________ Age____ Occupation________
Names and ages of children_______________________________

Educational Background

High school completed grade_____

Higher Education _______________

___Yes ___No If incomplete high school, do you have a GED?

___Yes ___No Do you speak any language other than English?

Language(s) spoken: ___________________

__Speak Some __Fairly Fluent __Very Fluent

Describe any vocational or medical training you have had, any other education beyond high school, or any special skills you have:

____

____

____

In a few words, please describe your Christian experience, your interest in missions, and why you desire to serve at CHO Haiti (you may use back of this sheet):___________________________

____

____

____

____

____

____

____

____

What areas of work at CHO are you most interested in?________

____

How long would you like to stay in Haiti?__________________

How do you expect to raise funds for your transportation and support? (NOTE: You should be prepared to give CHO $10/day to cover cost of your room, board and laundry. Any exception to this policy must have prior approval from Mom Workman.)

____

____

I have read the information guideline sheets for CHO workers and agree to abide by the principles stated therein.

____________________________________ ____________________

Signature Date

Guidelines for CHO Workers

1. Please follow the instructions you've been given for your assigned job and keep the work hours you've been asked to take. Ask questions before you implement any new procedure or make any changes in the manner of doing your job. Changing any established format in the work habits of the Haitian staff members can cause great confusion and create many problems. Consult with Mom Workman or her designated staff person(s) concerning any new ideas which you believe would make the work easier or help the ministry in general.

2. Do not accept invitations from any Haitian to go anyplace outside the orphanage without prior approval of Mom Workman. When walking back and forth between the orphanage and the Extension (where missionary staff are housed), always walk with another staff member until you are known by the people in the neighborhood and you know whom you can trust. Until you are oriented to the culture and have learned how to get around by public transport, do not leave the immediate area around the compound without having another staff member with you.

3. Do not, under any circumstances, visit a voodoo compound or a voodoo ceremony. This is strictly against CHO policy.

4. CHO workers must not smoke or drink alcoholic beverages at any time — either on or off the CHO compound.

5. Do not offer gifts or money to any Haitian without prior approval of Mom Workman. If you observe a

genuine need on the part of a worker or someone in the neighborhood and want to help, check with Mom or the person in charge. CHO has a system for providing assistance for needy people, so we ask you to work with the system.

6. Do not request special favors from or offer to pay for routine services of any kind for any of the Haitian workers without prior approval of Mom Workman or the person in charge.

7. Purpose in your heart to be loving and flexible at all times. Many times you may not understand the motives behind some of the decisions and policies of CHO, or the instructions you receive. Please pray that God will give an understanding as you strive to go along with the flow of things.

8. Please respect other missionary staff members living in the Extension by cleaning up after yourself in the kitchen, leaving the bathroom neat after each use and keeping the volume low when talking with someone or playing a radio or tape player. Some staff workers work the night shift and must sleep in the daytime. Please show them your consideration.

9. Please turn off lights and fans when you leave your room to help us keep our utility bill as low as possible.

10. The day begins at 5:00 a.m. each day with a one-hour prayer meeting in the chapel, led by Mom Workman or a designated person in her absence. You are encouraged to participate in this prayer meeting with other missionary and Haitian staff members and believers in the community.

11. The gate to the orphanage is locked at 11:00 p.m. each night and unlocked the next morning before 5:00 a.m. A gatekeeper is on duty at the gate at all times.

12. Remember that you are loved, appreciated, highly prized and precious to Mom Workman, as well as to all the other staff members. All decisions concerning your activities while serving at CHO in Haiti are made with your best interest in mind, and are based on prior knowledge and experience in working within the Haitian culture.

13. As a member of the ministry group here in Haiti, your very life will be a constant testimony for or against Jesus Christ, for or against CHO and for or against your own country. It is ever so important that you take note how you live, what you say, how you act and even how you dress in front of the Haitian people.

14. For clothing we suggest lightweight, light colored, cotton blend, drip dry fabric. For women we insist that you wear dresses or skirts and blouses...no pants, culottes or shorts, and no bare-topped sundresses. For men we insist that you wear a shirt at all times when you are working or are in the public. Pants that are cut knee length are acceptable for work and casual wear but not short shorts. For your own safety, shoes or sandals should be worn at all times. For church services, men should wear long trousers and a shirt; if you are ministering in a service, you should wear a necktie. Ladies, wear modest summer clothing for church services. (Of course swimsuits are allowed when you are at the beach or swimming pool, but do take along a cover-up.)

15. You may want to bring a supply of snack foods and items such as canned meats, nuts, wrapped candy,

popcorn, instant coffee, sugar substitutes, creamer, Tang, Koolaid mix, etc. Also bring vitamins, any medications you may need and a supply of toiletry items. These items can be purchased in Haiti, but prices are high because the goods are imported, expensive and have a long shelf life. Please do not use food or toiletry items belonging to another missionary without asking permission.

I pray your time of service in Haiti will be a rewarding experience for you and the Haitian people whom you come to serve. We thank God for your willingness to help.

Eleanor Workman

Tips on Getting Along With Missionaries and Nationals

John Garlock

1. Respect seniority. The older worker probably has a good reason for doing things the way he/she does. They haven't explained it to you. Don't suggest what you think is a better way of doing things until you've observed the work for quite awhile, and have earned the respect of your co-workers.

2. Accept advice, at least temporarily, even if you don't understand why it's been given. "Stay away from so-and-so," or "Do this right away" is probably a good idea. Later you can make your own evaluations as to what is important, but be careful of making snap judgments.

3. Ask for help. It's usually not resented, provided it does not require too much of the other person's time. The missionary or national worker with whom you are dealing would like to feel he is important to you. Don't be too proud to admit you need him or her.

4. Learn the "history" of the work and of the other missionaries. Knowing something of the past helps you get perspective on the present and on the future.

5. Avoid a contrasting lifestyle; i.e., don't be too different from others (this includes adapting to local food, meal schedules, etc.). Japanese proverb: "It's the nail that sticks up that gets pounded." And don't flaunt any luxuries you may have.

6. Avoid making commitments without consultation. There may be a good reason why you *shouldn't* accept an invitation, even if it is to minister somewhere.

You can easily be tainted by your associations or inadvertently get drawn into a problem.

7. Maintain regular communication with other missionaries. If possible, set up a regular schedule of shared breakfast on Thursdays, or phoning every Saturday morning, or some such thing.

8. Try for friendships, not for partnerships, by: a) Showing appreciation by expressing thanks, b) Helping with the other fellow's work; it pays, c) Doing favors; being supportive, d) Giving gifts, not expensive, but thoughtful, e) Praying for fellow missionaries and national workers.

9. *Never* criticize another missionary to a national worker. You may lose the respect not only of the missionary, but of the national worker as well. By the same token, don't criticize a national worker to a missionary. First of all, pray about problems and conflicts, asking the Lord to show you the problem from *His* perspective. Then try to work things out by talking and praying together with the person concerned. Many cultures place high value on "family loyalty."

Adoption Information

In the pages of this book, you have seen time and again that God has worked miracles to bring children into the families who were right for them. But the blessing goes both ways. We have seen so many times that the parents' joy, as well as the bonds between the new parents and the children they adopt, are more wonderful and stronger than words can adequately describe. CHO is interested in securing homes with Christian families for their beautiful, orphaned children.

As a prospective adoptive parent, you must prayerfully consider the role you would be playing in the life of one of these children. We will unite with you in prayer as you consider the child who will share your life, home, heart and your love. Therefore, we are asking that you complete the enclosed questionnaire. Upon receipt of it, we will send you further information on the available children and pictures of one who may become your very own son or daughter.

There is very much to be considered in an international adoption, as the process differs from adoptions in the States. While CHO is not an adoption agency (we house and care for the children until they are adopted), we would be very glad to act as the liaison to take documents to and out of Haiti for you. Ultimately, we will be happy to bring your child out of the country when the process is completed. However, we are hopeful that you can arrange to go and meet and bring your child home, which would help the child make an easier adjustment to his/her new home.

Please feel free to contact us at anytime regarding adoption. If you are unable to begin adoption proceedings at this time, we hope you will sponsor (meet by mail and photo) a child on a monthly basis to help meet his or her needs. You can support an infant for $15 per month or a school-age child for $25 per month. More information is available upon request.

International Adoption Requirements

The following information will give you an idea of what is needed to meet the requirements of an international adoption:

1. You will need to obtain a copy of the *I-6OO Form* from your local office of Immigration and Naturalization. At that time, also inquire about what will satisfy your state's Immigration and Naturalization requirements for completing an international adoption. Stay in close touch with the Immigration office throughout the adoption and after the child comes home to you to assist you in filing the appropriate follow-up documents.
2. The following documents in *triplicate*. All copies must be *notarized*.
   a. Birth Certificate for both husband and wife.
   b. Marriage Certificate.
   c. Security check.
   d. Character reference.
   e. Police identification — with fingerprints for both parents.
   f. Statement of educational background.
   g. Religious affiliation.
   h. Record of financial security, savings, investments, insurance (life, hospitalization, home).
   i. Work record, how long employed, where, position, salary.

3. A homestudy completed by a licensed, certified state, local, or private adoption agency.
4. A statement of why you would like to adopt a Haitian child (250 words or more).

The cost will be about $1,500 - $2,000 inclusive of $1,000 for the attorney's fee in Haiti and $500 for your child's visa, passport, physical and one-way ticket airfare from Haiti. If you request someone from CHO to bring the child home, their airfare would be additional. We strongly recommend that you, as the adoptive parent, make the trip to Haiti to meet and spend a little time with your child getting to know you. This will ensure a smoother transition for your child.

Adoption Questionnaire

Please fill in where applicable and return to P. O. Box 634545, Margate, FL 33063-4545. This completed form will remain on file with CHO and help us to assist you during your adoption. Please attach additional paper for responses where necessary.

1. Name________________________Date of birth__________
   (Adopting father) (first) (middle) (last)

2. Name________________________Date of birth__________
   (Adopting mother) (first) (middle) (last)

3. Address____
   (Street) (Apartment #)

   ____
   (City) (State) (Zip)

4. Telephone # (___)__________ Business # (___)__________

5. Religious Identification ______________________________

6. Employment of father:
   Occupation ______________________________________
   Employer _______________________________________
   Address ____
   Phone ______________________

   Employment of mother:
   Occupation ______________________________________
   Employer _______________________________________
   Address ____
   Phone ______________________

7. Children:
   Name Birthdate Own or Adopted

   ____
   ____
   ____
   ____
   ____

8. Others living in the home:
   Name Age Relationship
   ____
   ____
   ____
   ____

9. Have you an active application for adoption with another source?
   ____
   If so, where?______________________________

10. In what type of child are you interested?
    Age ____________ Sex ____________
    Other preferences __________________________

11. How, when and why did you begin to consider adoption?
    ____
    ____
    ____
    ____
    ____
    ____

12. What have been some of your experiences with children?
    ____
    ____
    ____
    ____
    ____
    ____

13. What do you do for recreation, outside activities, hobbies, etc.?
    ____
    ____
    ____
    ____
    ____
    ____

14. Please attach a second sheet of paper answering the follow ing question in 250 words or more. Please retain copies of your reply, as the same statements will be included when you submit your completed adoption packet of information.

    Why we (I) want to adopt a Haitian child:

________________________________ ________________

Signature of father Date

________________________________ ________________

Signature of mother Date

Upon receipt of your questionnaire, we will review it and get back with you if there are any problems. We will assist you during the adoption process by answering your questions for whatever applies to CHO and on the children who are available for adoption and in need of good homes.

Please be assured that we are here to assist you and that we are praying with you as you embark upon parenthood with the Lord's guidance.

Sincerely,

Eleanor Workman
Founder and President
Christian Haitian Outreach, Inc.

For more information on
Christian Haitian Outreach,
write:

For shipping boxes of packaged gifts:

Eleanor Workman
Christian Haitian Outreach, Inc.
6347 N.W. 22nd Court
Margate, FL 33063-2216
(954/972-3674) PHONE

For mailing funds/ correspondence:

Eleanor Workman
Christian Haitian Outreach, Inc.
P. O. Box 634545
Margate, FL 33063-4545
(954/970-6840) FAX